Combating Crime on the Dark Web

Learn how to access the dark web safely and not fall victim to cybercrime

Nearchos Nearchou

BIRMINGHAM—MUMBAI

Combating Crime on the Dark Web

Copyright © 2023 Packt Publishing

Group Product Manager: Mohd Riyan Khan
Publishing Product Manager: Mohd Riyan Khan
Senior Editor: Arun Nadar
Technical Editor: Nithik Cheruvakodan
Copy Editor: Safis Editing
Project Coordinator: Ashwin Kharwa
Proofreader: Safis Editing
Indexer: Subalakshmi Govindhan
Production Designer: Shyam Sundar Korumilli
Senior Marketing Coordinator: Marylou De Mello

First published: Jan 2023

Production reference: 1050123

Published by Packt Publishing Ltd.
Livery Place
35 Livery Street
Birmingham
B3 2PB, UK.

ISBN 978-1-80323-498-4

www.packtpub.com

To my parents, who always stand next to me.

Contributors

About the author

Nearchos Nearchou is a determined person and 1st Class BSc (Hons) Computer Science and MSc Cyber Security graduate. He is a big tech-lover and spent several years exploring new innovations in the IT field. Driven by his passion for learning, he is pursuing a career in the cybersecurity world. He is passionate about learning new skills and information that can be used for further personal and career development. As well as working individually, he enjoys working as part of a team in order to deliver projects on time and to the highest possible standard.

Throughout the whole process of working on this book, I have received a great deal of support and assistance from various people.

I would first like to thank the Packt team, whose expertise was crucial in formulating the research question and methodology. Their guidance, support, and encouragement have been invaluable throughout this study. Additionally, their insightful feedback pushed me to sharpen my way of thinking and advance the level of my work.

Furthermore, I would like to show my appreciation to my family for their support during the writing process. My family's persistence and trust have encouraged me throughout this journey, and without them, I would not have been able to complete this book.

About the reviewer

Sion Retzkin has been in cybersecurity for almost two decades, performing both technical- and business-related roles, such as pentesting, product management, sales, pre-sales and more. He has also been the CISO in three companies. He began his career in cybersecurity in the IDF and currently works at Pentera, the global leader in automated security validation, as head of channel enablement EMEA & APAC. He is also the author of the book *Hands-On Dark Web Analysis*.

Disclaimer

The information within this book is intended to be used only in an ethical manner. Do not use any information from the book if you do not have written permission from the owner of the equipment. If you perform illegal actions, you are likely to be arrested and prosecuted to the full extent of the law. Packt Publishing does not take any responsibility if you misuse any of the information contained within the book. The information herein must only be used while testing environments with properly written authorizations from the appropriate persons responsible.

Table of Contents

Part 2: The Dark Web's Ecosystem and Major Crimes

3

4

5

6

Cyberterrorism on the Dark Web   67

Part 3: Efforts to Combat Crimes on the Dark Web

7

Efforts for Combating Crime on the Dark Web   81

8

System for Combating Crime on the Dark Web   93

Discussion and Evaluation   105

Preface

The Dark Web is the content of the Internet that has been intentionally concealed and users need special software and authorization to access it. The main Dark Web access tool is Tor Browser, and it works by hiding your IP address through the onion routing technology. The Dark Web can be used for legitimate purposes, that is, news leaks, whistleblowing, anonymous browsing, and to conduct illegal activities related to narcotics distribution, human trafficking, child pornography, terrorism, and many others.

This book will give you an opportunity to understand how Dark Web crime works and how to avoid the risks associated with it. You will learn how to safely access this hidden part of the Internet and not fall victim to it. Finally, you will learn how to protect your personal data and how to build a strong private online presence.

> **Disclaimer**
>
> Some of the content in this book may be sensitive and may or may not be the opinions, ideas, or beliefs of the author who collected the materials or their informants. The information in this book is for general informational purposes only. Packt makes no representation or warranty, express or implied. Your use of the book is solely at your own risk. This book may contain links to third-party content, which we do not warrant, endorse, or assume liability for.

Who this book is for

This book is targeted at cybersecurity enthusiasts or anyone who is interested in learning about this dark part of the internet. The book mainly focuses on preventing crimes on the Dark Web and is written in a simple way so that literally anyone can understand it.

What this book covers

Chapter 1, An Introduction to Cybercrime, covers a wide range of topics related to cybercrime. It starts with the main types of cybercrime and how you can protect yourself from it. Subsequently, it describes the evolution of cybercrime and how it can affect people's lives. Finally, the chapter concludes with the three main levels of the internet and the tools you can use to access the Dark Web.

Chapter 2, An Introduction to the Dark Web, starts with a history of the Dark Web and how it has evolved through the years. Additionally, this chapter describes in detail the three main tools used to access the Dark Web, which are the Tor Browser, the **Invisible Internet Project** (**I2P**), and Freenet software. Finally, the chapter explains the world of cryptocurrencies and how they are used to conduct illegal activities and transactions on the Dark Web.

Chapter 3, Drug Markets on the Dark Web, goes into detail about the world of narcotics on the Dark Web. The chapter covers a wide range of topics, including the drug market's ecosystem and what enables transactions between buyers and sellers. Additionally, the chapter describes the ways law enforcement, the private sector, and the public use to fight the Dark Web drug markets.

Chapter 4, Child Pornography on the Dark Web, covers in detail the aspects of this heinous crime. The chapter discusses the issues surrounding Dark Web child pornography and explains the difference between child abuse/exploitation terms. Additionally, the chapter describes the behaviors of pedophiles on the Dark Web and what techniques they use to conduct their illegal activities. The chapter concludes with the various ways law enforcement and the private sector use to detect and capture child offenders on the Dark Web.

Chapter 5, Human Trafficking on the Dark Web, goes through the types of human trafficking and how traffickers behave on this hidden part of the Internet. The chapter covers the tactics and methods offenders use when exploiting vulnerable humans on the Dark Web. Subsequently, the chapter covers the impact Dark Web human trafficking has on society and the ways authorities use it to capture offenders.

Chapter 6, Cyberterrorism on the Dark Web, covers the issues surrounding terrorism on the Dark Web. The chapter starts with an explanation of the various types of cyber terrorists. Next, the chapter describes the reasons why terrorists use the Dark Web and how they can benefit from it. Finally, the chapter concludes with the methods law enforcement uses to prosecute terrorists on the Dark Web.

Chapter 7, Efforts for Combating Crime on the Dark Web, describes the various ways and tools law enforcement and the private sector use to mitigate crime on the Dark Web. The chapter goes into detail about honeypot traps and sting operations, two widely used cybersecurity disruption methods. Additionally, it covers the three best tools (traffic confirmation attack, **open source intelligence** (**OSINT**), and the MEMEX project) to effectively combat crime on the Dark Web.

Chapter 8, System for Combating Crime on the Dark Web, describes in detail an efficient system for combating crime on the Dark Web. It utilizes the collaborative approach and suggests that all entities must come together to achieve better results.

Chapter 9, Discussion and Evaluation, provides an overview of the overall research done on crimes that happen on the Dark Web.

Conventions used

There are a number of text conventions used throughout this book.

`Code in text`: Indicates code words in text, database table names, folder names, filenames, file extensions, pathnames, dummy URLs, user input, and Twitter handles. Here is an example: "Specifically, websites accessed through the Tor Browser have the `.onion` domain suffix, a special top-level domain name referring to an anonymous onion service."

Get in touch

Feedback from our readers is always welcome.

General feedback: If you have questions about any aspect of this book, email us at `customercare@packtpub.com` and mention the book title in the subject of your message.

Errata: Although we have taken every care to ensure the accuracy of our content, mistakes do happen. If you have found a mistake in this book, we would be grateful if you would report this to us. Please visit `www.packtpub.com/support/errata` and fill in the form.

Piracy: If you come across any illegal copies of our works in any form on the internet, we would be grateful if you would provide us with the location address or website name. Please contact us at `copyright@packt.com` with a link to the material.

If you are interested in becoming an author: If there is a topic that you have expertise in and you are interested in either writing or contributing to a book, please visit `authors.packtpub.com`.

Share Your Thoughts

Once you've read *Combating Crime on the Dark Web*, we'd love to hear your thoughts! Scan the QR code below to go straight to the Amazon review page for this book and share your feedback.

`https://packt.link/r/1803234989`

Your review is important to us and the tech community and will help us make sure we're delivering excellent quality content.

Download a free PDF copy of this book

Thanks for purchasing this book!

Do you like to read on the go but are unable to carry your print books everywhere? Is your eBook purchase not compatible with the device of your choice?

Don't worry, now with every Packt book you get a DRM-free PDF version of that book at no cost.

Read anywhere, any place, on any device. Search, copy, and paste code from your favorite technical books directly into your application.

The perks don't stop there, you can get exclusive access to discounts, newsletters, and great free content in your inbox daily

Follow these simple steps to get the benefits:

1. Scan the QR code or visit the link below

https://packt.link/free-ebook/9781803234984

2. Submit your proof of purchase
3. That's it! We'll send your free PDF and other benefits to your email directly

Part 1: Introduction to Cybercrime and Dark Web's History

In *Part 1*, the reader will understand the various types of cybercrime and when cybercrime started. Also, the reader will understand how the Dark Web evolved throughout the years, and the impact it has on people's lives.

This part has the following chapters:

An Introduction to Cybercrime

The internet is widely regarded as the epitome of never-ending innovation and creativity. It is considered the most fascinating, wild, and phenomenal creation in the history of humanity. According to a study, 95 percent of all the world's information is digitized and accessible on the internet. If you even begin to think about how big the internet is, your brain might start to hurt. One way to answer this question is to consider the total amount of data held by the biggest online **service providers** (**SPs**)—that is, Google, Facebook, Amazon, and Microsoft. *Science Focus* estimates that these tech giants collectively store at least 1,200 petabytes of data. That is 1.2 million terabytes, which is equal to approximately 1,200,000,000,000,000,000 bytes (*Mitchell, 2021*).

If information is power in the digital/online age (and it is), then Google has the right to claim that it is the most influential company in the world. It dominates almost every sector it is getting into, as it has collected, digitized, arranged, and presented more information than any other company in the world's history. According to reports, Google owns more than 90 percent of the worldwide search market. More than 2 trillion Google searches are made every year (*BroadbandSearch, 2021*). To put this in perspective, that works out to more than 5 billion searches every day, 228 million every hour, 3 million every minute, and 63,000 every second.

This chapter gives an overview of the broad research, with a particular focus on cybercrime and the Dark Web. Understanding what cybercrime is, the various types, and how to protect yourself from it will help to keep our society running and stay safe online. Subsequently, the chapter briefly discusses two popular Dark Web access tools (**The Onion Router** (**TOR**) browser and the **Invisible Internet Project** (**I2P**)). Specifically, this chapter covers the following topics:

- Classification of major cybercrimes
- Types of cyberattacks
- Evolution of cybercrime
- The internet's three primary levels
- Dark Web access tools

Classification of major cybercrimes

While the digital dimension may (on different levels) improve people's lives, it leaves them vulnerable to emerging threats, potentially with severe implications. The internet has acted as a new pathway for criminals to conduct their activities and launch attacks with relative obscurity. Cybercrime, also known as computer crime, refers to activities carried out by means of electronic devices, computers, or the internet to conduct illegal acts (*European Commission, 2021*). The majority of cybercrime is conducted by hackers or cybercriminals who are after financial gain. However, there are times when cybercrime tries to harm systems or networks for factors other than economic profit. The following list classifies three major categories of cybercrime:

- **Crimes against people**: This type of cybercrime aims to exploit human weaknesses, such as greed and naivety. It includes cyberstalking and harassment, extortion, defamation, credit card fraud, identity theft, human trafficking, distribution of child pornography, and so on (*Panda Security, 2021*).

- **Crimes against properties**: Some online crimes take place against properties, such as a computer or a server. This category of cybercrime includes cyber vandalism, virus transmission, cybersquatting, copyright infringement, cyber trespass, **distributed denial-of-service (DDoS)** attacks, and so on (*Swier Law Firm, 2021*).

- **Crimes against governments**: This kind of cybercrime may significantly impact a nation's sovereignty. Cybercrimes against a government include accessing confidential information, cyberwarfare, industrial espionage, network intrusions, cyberterrorism, and so on (*Arora, 2016*).

These days, cybercrime is running rampant. Warren Buffet, the billionaire mogul and philanthropist, believes that cybercrime is the number one issue with mankind and that cyberattacks are a much bigger threat to humanity than nuclear weapons. Mass attacks in cyberspace may even constitute a threat to international peace and security. *Cybersecurity Ventures* has estimated that the global cybercrime damage costs in 2025 will reach 10.5 trillion US dollars. The following figure shows the global cybercrime damage costs in 2021 (*Morgan, 2020*):

Global Cybercrime Damage Costs:

- $6 Trillion USD a Year.
- $500 Billion a Month.
- $115.4 Billion a Week.
- $16.4 Billion a Day.
- $684.9 Million a Hour.
- $684.9 Million a Minute.
- $190,000 a Second.

Figure 1.1 – Global cybercrime damage costs in 2021

With the pandemic (COVID-19) worsening and a fatigued remote workforce, the potential attack surface for cybercriminals has expanded dramatically. Cyber-related crimes continue to rise in scale and sophistication, and every day, essential services, businesses, and individuals become victims of malicious/harmful cyberattacks. Even though cyberattacks are not tangible as physical attacks are, they can be as impactful and devastating (*Lallie et al., 2021*). Some critical cybersecurity statistics and trends are set out here:

- The worldwide cybersecurity market is projected to reach 170.4 billion dollars in 2022 (*Contu et al., 2018*)
- Data breaches exposed 36 billion records in the first half of 2020 (*Goddijn, 2020*)
- 94 percent of malicious malware is delivered via email (*Phishing Box, 2019*)
- The average cost of a single data breach was 3.86 million US dollars in 2020 (*IBM Security, 2020*)
- Human error is to blame for 95 percent of cybersecurity breaches (*Hourihan, 2020*)
- In 2020, the average time to identify and contain a breach was 280 days (*IBM Security, 2020*)

As can be seen, taking cybersecurity seriously is of vital importance. Nowadays, data has become the most valuable asset in the world, and applying proper cybersecurity techniques may protect individuals and organizations from severe damage. You might be asking how to fight cybercrime given its ubiquity. Here are some wise recommendations for preventing cybercrime on your computer and your personal data:

- **Keep your operating system and software updated**: By maintaining an updated operating system and software, you can use the most recent security fixes to safeguard your machine.

- **Use antivirus software**: It's wise to use antivirus software to defend your PC from threats. You can scan, identify, and get rid of hazards with antivirus software before they become a problem. You may rest easy knowing that this protection is helping to safeguard your computer and your data against cybercrime. Maintain antivirus updates to get the best level of security.

- **Use strong passwords**: Use secure passwords that are impossible for anyone to guess, and don't save them elsewhere. Or, to make this simpler, use a trustworthy password manager to generate strong passwords at random.

- **Never open attachments in spam emails**: By clicking on links in spam emails, other unsolicited messages, or unknown websites, consumers can also become victims of cybercrime. To maintain your online safety, avoid doing this.

It is predicted that fast-paced changes in technology will cause a dramatic increase in cyberattacks. The following section describes the various types of cyberattacks, as well as how cybercrime has evolved throughout the years.

Types of cyberattacks

Digitalization is no longer part of a 1930s science-fiction movie. It is the past, present, and future of humankind. Digital transformation has positively changed almost every aspect of people's lives, but at the same time, it has brought with it many downsides. Cyberattacks have moved beyond harming computers, networks, and smartphones. Cybercriminals can attack literally anything with a heartbeat or an electronic pulse—for example, people, cars, refrigerators, railways, coffee machines, planes, baby monitors, power grids, drones, nuclear facilities, and so on.

A cyberattack refers to an action where a threat actor (attacker)—or a group of threat actors—attacks a computerized information system to steal, manipulate, alter, or destroy confidential data (*Pratt, 2021*). Because of the internet's global existence, hackers can be physically positioned anywhere in the world and still cause harm. While an attacker can use various techniques to penetrate a system, most cyberattacks rely on similar methods. Here is a list of the most common types of cyberattacks:

- **Phishing attack**: Phishing is a popular type of cyberattack where hackers send deceptive messages to unsuspected users. These messages appear to come from reputable sources—that is, friends, family, colleagues, banks, **internet service providers** (**ISPs**), and so on. Most phishing messages are delivered via email, and their goal is to do the following (*Phishing.org, 2021*):

    I.   Steal sensitive data such as credit/debit card numbers and login credentials.

    II.   Install malware on the victim's machine. The information obtained by the hackers can be used to steal the victim's identity, request money, or seek thrill/pleasure.

- **Malware attack**: Malware is a general term used to describe malicious software. This type of software is maliciously installed on a user's system (without their consent) and can perform various harmful tasks (*McAfee, 2021*). Spyware, ransomware, viruses, and worms are all types of malware attacks. Some forms of malware, such as ransomware, are designed to extort the victim in some way. This is done by purposefully encrypting their files and then demanding a fee to be paid to get the decryption key (*Ovide, 2020*).

- **DoS attack**: This type of attack works by using compromised devices to flood the targeted system with requests in order to disrupt its normal functioning. A DoS attack aims to make the system inaccessible to its intended users—that is, employees, clients, account holders, and others. Services affected may include emails, websites, and online banking. Also, attackers have the ability to use multiple compromised devices and cause even more harm. This is known as a DDoS attack (*Weisman, 2020*).

- **Structured Query Language (SQL) injection attack**: An SQL injection is considered the number one threat to web applications. It occurs when an attacker interferes with the queries an application (website) makes to its backend/server-side database. The hacker injects malicious code into the server and forces the server to display the user's database contents—for example, usernames, passwords, secret questions, and other information. An SQL injection is usually used to bypass authentication, disclose confidential information, or alter data (*Ping-Chen, 2011*).

Cyberattacks have a number of detrimental repercussions. When an attack is conducted, it may result in data breaches, which may cause data loss or manipulation. Companies suffer financial losses, a decrease in customer trust, and reputational harm. We employ cybersecurity to prevent cyberattacks. Networks, computers, and their component protection from unwanted digital access are known as cybersecurity.

Evolution of cybercrime

Cybercrime's evolution is easy to trace and coincides with the evolution of the internet itself. The internet provides a rich environment for criminal activity, ranging from vandalism to human trafficking to intellectual property theft.

The early years

Cybercrime first appeared in telecommunications and specifically with **phone phreaking**, which topped in the 1970s. Phone phreaking is a slang term coined to describe people who exploit hardware and frequency vulnerabilities of telephone signaling in order to make free calls (*Madsen, 2019*). Exploring telecommunication systems was not (and is not) illegal in and of itself, but exploiting this technique to get reduced phone rates is illegal. As landline communications became more secure, phone phreaking became much less common (*Brush, 2021*).

The time computer security turned real was around 8:30 p.m. on November 2, 1988. That night, a malicious virus, called Morris Worm, was propagating at a remarkable speed on the internet (*Federal Bureau of Investigation (FBI), 2018*). It was one of the first worms distributed via cyberspace and received mainstream attention. This kind of advanced software quickly transformed itself into the first large-scale DDoS attack. Systems around the globe were overwhelmed, and around 10 percent of the world's computers malfunctioned (*Seltzer, 2013*). Apart from privately owned computers, the worm took down computer servers in government facilities, hospitals, military bases, and so on. The actual damages were difficult to quantify, but it is estimated that the episode resulted in multi-million-dollar losses (*Capitol, 2018*).

The 1990s to 2000s

Although there was cybercrime at the beginning of the internet's creation, the first big surge of cybercrime came with phishing emails in the 1990s. Phishing is a type of social engineering attack (the practice of deceiving people to obtain valuable information). Phishing has made it easy to send numerous scams and/or viruses to people's email inboxes. Phishing emails often imitate a trusted source, such as a phone provider (*National Cyber Security Center UK, 2019*). They often include official-looking graphics, email addresses, and dummy websites to trick the user. Hackers send these kinds of emails to steal passwords and bank account numbers or to infect systems with viruses (*Alkhalil et al., 2021*).

Post-2000s

At the beginning of the 21st century, cybercrime was no longer controlled by criminals who were hacking computer systems just for fun or notoriety. The growth of the digital economy had changed the criminal landscape dramatically. Criminal gangs introduced a professional element into the world of cybercrime. Cybercrime had become so popular that well-organized networks of criminals started collaborating to pull off massive heists over the internet (*Heussner, 2011*). The following are some forms of cybercrime that appeared at the beginning of the millennium and still exist today:

- **Cyber extortion**: This type of cybercrime occurs when hackers steal and hold electronic files of an individual or a business until a demanded ransom is paid. Cyber extortion includes actions such as ransomware, email ransom campaigns, and DDoS attacks (*McMillan, 2017*).

- **Attacks against critical infrastructures**: Commonly attacked critical infrastructures include the energy, water supply, and health sectors. Transportation, public sector services, and telecommunications are also vulnerable. Such attacks draw the attention of several law enforcement authorities and pose an exaggerated risk (*Allianz, 2021*).

- **Cyberterrorism**: The potential damage cyberterrorism can cause provokes considerable alarm. Numerous cybersecurity experts, private companies, and politicians have publicized the possibility of criminals hacking into governmental and private computer systems. Cyberterrorism has the potential to cause severe damage to any country's military, financial, and service sectors (*Weimann, 2004*).

- **Online human trafficking**: This kind of cybercrime is a serious and growing problem. Digital technology and the internet are fueling worldwide growth in human trafficking. The internet provides traffickers with enormous potential to seek out and groom marginalized individuals. Sexual perpetrators can scan the internet to find vulnerable individuals of all ages (*Allen, 2019*).

- **Exploitation of children**: There is also a very real and nasty side to cybercrime. Almost every day, criminal gangs are being caught with child pornography. Never before has it been so easy for pedophiles to come into contact with children. This kind of material can be found all over the internet, including the notorious Dark Web (*Broadhurst and Ball, 2021*).

Cybercrimes are a global threat and are more rampant than ever in the year 2022. With the COVID-19 pandemic worsening and a fatigued workforce, the potential attack surface for cybercriminals has increased in size dramatically. Cybercriminals and the sophisticated technologies they use are often based abroad, making international cooperation between agencies essential. Apart from disrupting the current generation of cybercriminals, it's of vital importance to prevent young individuals from slipping into cybercrime. Regional organized crime units, as well as international law enforcement—for example, the FBI, Interpol, and Europol—must encourage young people with cyber skills to use their knowledge wisely and avoid any cyber-related illegal activities.

The internet's three primary levels

The internet is an immense archive that contains vast amounts of data. Web data extraction, also known as web scraping or web harvesting, is one of the most advanced tools for gathering information from around the internet. Such tools can help companies with the following:

1. Gaining market and competitive intelligence

2. Keeping up to date with changes to compliance and regulation terms

3. Staying abreast with developments in their industry

This level of data extraction provides access to a large repository of content that is usually hidden (*Cerami, 2017*). The following screenshot shows the internet's primary levels (*How big is the Internet, 2018*):

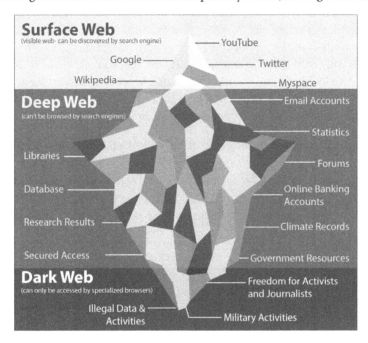

Figure 1.2 – The three primary levels of the internet

The internet consists of three levels: the Surface Web, the Deep Web, and the Dark Web. Each one of them is unique and is being used for specific things:

- **The Surface Web**: The Surface Web, also known as the *Indexed Web*, *Visible Web*, or *Lightnet*, is anything you can find on the regular World Wide Web. It is readily available to the general public and the primary entry point for most people. This portion of the internet consists of websites indexed by regular search engines—that is, Google, Bing, Yahoo, and so on. It has only around 5 percent of what is available on the internet. The Surface Web can be accessed using standard web browsers that do not require special configuration—for example, Mozilla Firefox, Microsoft Edge, Google Chrome, Opera, Brave, and so on (*Center for Internet Security, 2021*).

- **The Deep Web**: The Deep Web is below the Surface Web and accounts for approximately 90 percent of all internet traffic. It contains most of the internet's data, and standard search engines do not index its contents. In fact, the Deep Web is so large that it is impossible to precisely estimate how many pages or websites it has. Specifically, it includes websites that require authentication to access them—that is, usernames and passwords. Most of the Deep Web's contents are related to academic journals, private databases, and medical records. The Deep Web also includes the portion of the internet known as the Dark Web (*Kaspersky, 2021*).

- **The Dark Web**: The Dark Web includes sites that cannot be found by conventional search engines and can only be accessed via specialized browsers. When compared to the Surface Web, the Dark Web is significantly smaller, and it is considered a part of the Deep Web. Using the screenshot shown earlier, the Dark Web is at the bottom tip of the submerged iceberg. To navigate this portion of the internet, you need special programs such as the TOR browser. This program will connect you to an overlay network that will *mask your IP address*, making your online activity highly anonymous. The Dark Web can be used for legitimate purposes as well as to conduct criminal activities related to fraud, weapons, drugs, child pornography, assassinations, human trafficking, zoophilia, and so on (*Guccione, 2021*).

To sum up, the following are some significant variations between the Dark Web, the Deep Web, and the Surface Web:

FEATURES	SURFACE WEB	DEEP WEB	DARK WEB
Accessibility	Freely accessible	Requires login credentials and a website's exact URL	Requires a special browser and a website's exact URL
Browser-friendliness	Can be visited using any browser	Can be visited using any browser	Can only be visited using a special browser
Search engine-friendliness	Can be found on a search engine (for example, Google, Yahoo, Bing, and others)	Can't usually be found on search engines	Can't be found on search engines at all
Examples	Google, Facebook, Amazon, VPNOverview	Confidential databases and employee pages of corporations, universities, and organizations	Black markets, Tor-exclusive email services

Figure 1.3 – Surface Web versus Deep Web versus Dark Web

In conclusion, you must realize that the Dark Web is not a place you decide to visit one morning. Understanding that the majority of ISPs hunt for users of TOR-like services—the most typical entrance point—requires some thought. Use one of the many tutorials available to you if you really want to access the Dark Web to learn how to set it up and where to begin.

Dark Web access tools

The Dark Web is often confused with the Deep Web, but it is essential to understand that these two are different entities. In simple terms, the Dark Web is a unique portion of the Deep Web, approximately 0.01 percent of it. There are a few distinguishing characteristics that a website must meet to be considered a Dark Web site. A Dark Web site must only be able to be accessed anonymously through a specialized browser such as TOR, Freenet, or I2P. Specifically, websites accessed through the TOR browser have the `.onion` domain suffix, a special top-level domain name referring to an anonymous onion service (*Porup, 2019*). The following screenshot shows what the full onion URL of the popular search engine DuckDuckGo looks like (*DeepOnionWeb, 2019*):

http://3g2upl4pq6kufc4m.onion

the hostname is randomly generated from the Tor software to create a hidden service

.onion is a domain suffix reachable only via the Tor network

Figure 1.4 – DuckDuckGo onion URL

TOR is the most popular and most used Dark Web browser. As of October 2022, it has approximately 2 million users worldwide (*TOR Metrics, 2022*). A simplistic interpretation of TOR is that of an open source browser, which is actually an adaption of the Firefox browser. In a TOR network, thousands of volunteers around the world run relays (servers) that route traffic. The traffic is relayed and encrypted multiple times as it passes over the TOR network (*TOR Project, 2021*). Only a handful of alternative technologies can match TOR's sophisticated features. The fact that all TOR users look alike on the internet makes TOR one of the most elite cyberspace technologies of all time.

Another popular Dark Web tool is **I2P**. I2P is an anonymous network like TOR, and it utilizes the *end-to-end encryption* standard. This standard is a secure communication method that stops other people from accessing packets of data while they are transmitted from one end system to another (*Astolfi, Kroese, and Oorschot, 2015*). The main difference between TOR and I2P is that I2P does not rely on a centralized database of server nodes, as it uses *garlic routing* rather than TOR's *onion routing*. Garlic routing is an improved browsing technology and an extension of onion routing, and like garlic cloves, it works by encrypting multiple messages together into a layered encryption standard. The garlic technology increases data speed and makes it more difficult for attackers to perform traffic analysis. I2P's decentralized approach has two significant advantages: **better scalability** and **no trusted central party** (*Ali et al., 2016*).

Due to the COVID-19 pandemic, more of people's everyday activities have taken place at home. They include distance education, virtual offices, digital entertainment, online shopping, and doctor visits. However, this problem has increased the risk of attacks through the internet. The FBI stated that the number of cyberattacks reported from January to May 2020 was nearly the same as the number of cyberattacks for the entire year of 2019.

Several factors can affect potential victims' vulnerabilities, including the following:

- Individual behavior
- Online activities

- Personal traits
- Attitudes about technology

It's thus crucial for mental health services to know about the possible effects of cyberattacks and patient risks. This scenario can include the impact of internet-based mental health services during the coronavirus outbreak.

Summary

The Dark Web is the content of the internet that can only be accessed by using specialized browsers. Users must use specific software, configurations, and authorization to browse this hidden part of the World Wide Web. Responses to Dark Web crime are more efficient, coordinated, and effective when they are collaborative and multidisciplinary in their problem-solving. By thoroughly investigating the Dark Web's ecosystem, this book will propose and analyze a cross-sector system for combating crime on the Dark Web more effectively. The next chapter extensively reviews the existing literature in order to identify gaps and answer the research question. Great emphasis is given to the Dark Web's most common types of cybercrimes as well as to the Dark Web's ecosystem.

2

An Introduction to the Dark Web

This chapter covers a wide range of topics about the Dark Web. It starts with an introduction to the history of the Dark Web, as well as how this hidden part of the internet evolved throughout the years. Subsequently, this chapter describes in detail the three most used tools for accessing the Dark Web, which are **The Onion Router** (**TOR**) network, the **Invisible Internet Project** (**I2P**), and the Freenet software. Finally, this chapter concludes with a description of cryptocurrencies and how they are used to conduct criminal activities on the Dark Web. The main objective of this chapter is to give an overview of how the Dark Web works and how regular people can access it. Additionally, it helps to understand how the combination of Dark Web accessing tools along with the use of cryptocurrencies allows criminals to expand their activities on the internet. Specifically, this chapter covers the following topics:

- History of the Dark Web
- The TOR browser and other Dark Web technologies
- The use of cryptocurrencies on the Dark Web

History of the Dark Web

The internet has changed significantly since the 1990s when it first became widely available. The growth of the so-called Dark Web is one of the most divisive shifts. Though some people may think that the Dark Web is a discovery of the 21st century, its history dates back much further. The idea of an anonymous secure network stretches all the way back to the 1960s. In that decade, the **Advanced Research Projects Agency Network** (**ARPANET**) was created. This experimental network was the beginning of the internet and, after a few years, the Dark Web. ARPANET started as a platform for academic use, but it quickly became a valuable tool for the military of the US (*Featherly, 2021*).

The term **Darknet** was introduced in the 1970s to designate networks isolated from ARPANET (that period's internet). In simple words, a Darknet is a set of interconnected networks wherein all network traffic is hidden. Thus, anyone can browse a Darknet, leaving little to no traces (*Mirea, Wang,* and

Jung, 2018). For some people, Darknets are a means to achieve ultimate online anonymity, while for others, these networks are no more than tools to express their criminogenic desires. Darknets are used for various reasons (*Finklea, 2017*), such as the following:

- Ensuring privacy and freedom of expression

- Making it easier to engage in criminal activities—for example, human trafficking, fraud, drug distribution, contract killings, modern slavery, and so on

- File sharing (personal files, child pornography, confidential information, illegal software, and others)

- Protecting dissidents from political reprisal

- Trading of illegal goods on Darknet markets—for example, weapon distribution

- Whistleblowing and news leaks

- Purchasing of illegal goods or services

- Enabling users controlled by oppressive governments to access content that might be geographically blocked

The issue of keeping sensitive and illegal material grew significantly with the advent of the modern web, which was highlighted by the establishment of the **Internet Protocol** (**IP**) suite in 1982. The informational equivalent of tax havens, physical data havens were used in early solutions. These data havens, mostly hosted in the Caribbean, promised to store everything from illegal pornographic sites to casino data (*McCormick, 2013*).

In the 1990s, the internet started going mainstream, and advances in file compression coupled with falling storage costs set off an explosion of Darknet activity. It was only a matter of time before other criminal operations started to emerge as people realized they could easily get whatever they wanted whenever they wanted via the internet (*McCormick, 2013*).

The 1960s-1990s era brought attention to the rising need for private internet connection away from the government's prying eyes. Even while the TOR project's development started in the 1990s, it wasn't until TOR's formal release in 2002 that it truly spurred the rise of the Dark Web. TOR was released with the intention of remaining a free and open piece of software. This was done to ensure that everyone could easily access the software and that it would rely on a decentralized network for optimum security and anonymity (*Newman, 2019*).

Private networks such as TOR were made available, which led to the emergence of multiple Dark Web sites and a subsequent following. Many hidden websites were initially created to assist people in fighting censorship while living under authoritarian regimes. However, the lure of having a private space online led to a massive rise in the number of dark websites providing illegal content. The following screenshot demonstrates the development of the Dark Web over time (*Kastner, 2020*):

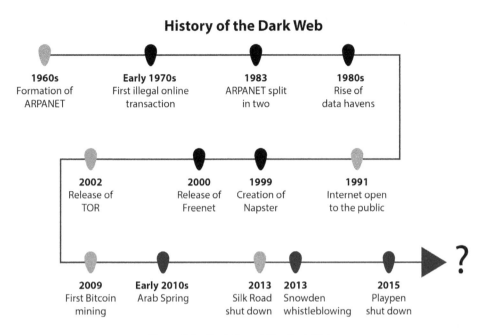

Figure 2.1 – Evolution of the Dark Web

Cybercrimes committed on the Dark Web are comparable to physical crimes. The massive scale, complex environment, and anonymity offered by Dark Web hidden services, however, are crucial challenges to catching offenders. Today, the Dark Web hosts a vast range of sites and forums related to illegal and unethical purposes, from counterfeit goods, illicit markets for drugs, human trafficking, and contract killings to extremist sites, money laundering, and forums for distributing child sexual abuse material. All these activities are legitimate targets for law enforcement. These activities are easy to conduct, and because of TOR's encryption mechanisms, it is much more challenging to prevent these and prosecute them. However, the Dark Web is not used only by criminals. Activists and political dissidents, law enforcement and police authorities, journalists, and the army also take advantage of the anonymity and security offered by encryption (*Hadjimatheou, 2020*). Although software such as TOR helps to hide users' activity, researchers and cybersecurity professionals constantly create means by which specific Dark Web services, websites, and individuals could be detected and *de-anonymized* (*Finklea, 2017*).

The TOR browser and other Dark Web technologies

The overall concept of Dark Web technologies is about routing users' data through several intermediate servers (nodes). Only a following server on the path, which leads to the exit server, is capable of decrypting the transmitted data. This type of technology ensures anonymity and protects the users' identities. This section covers the three main Dark Web technologies, which are the TOR network, IP2, and the Freenet software.

How the TOR network works

The TOR browser is a low-latency circuit-based anonymous communication platform. As with other low-latency anonymity networks, TOR aims to make it difficult for attackers to correlate communication patterns or correlate multiple connections to or from a single user. It works on the internet, requires no special modifications or kernel privileges, requires little coordination or synchronization between nodes, and provides a reasonable trade-off between efficiency, anonymity, and usability. TOR aims to provide online anonymity by using a unique architectural network topology, which involves thousands of nodes deployed worldwide. If hackers gain access to a node (relay), they can see the traffic that runs through it, but they cannot see where it comes from or goes next. TOR is a highly developed privacy technology, but it also has a number of drawbacks, some of which offset its cybersecurity benefits. The following are some drawbacks of using TOR:

- **Slow speeds**: Web traffic is encrypted and routed across a number of network nodes using onion routing, which is wonderful for privacy but slows down performance when compared to other browsers. Although there are ways to speed up TOR, speeds cannot be greatly increased.

- **Stigma**: TOR has unfortunately come to represent lawlessness on the Dark Web. Governments and ISPs might keep track of who uses the browser. TOR might offer those who desire privacy the exact opposite.

- **Blocking**: Some network operators obstruct TOR. Additionally, some websites monitor and restrict traffic from TOR exit nodes, but employing TOR bridges or a **virtual private network** (**VPN**) will allow you to conceal node usage.

- **Vulnerabilities**: Despite the fact that TOR is intended to maintain anonymity, the onion network is exposed at the entry and exit nodes. Your data is susceptible to interception and your IP address can be made public because internet traffic is not encrypted at these points.

The anonymous nature of TOR, along with the use of cryptocurrencies—for example, Bitcoin, Ethereum, Monero, and so on—makes TOR one of the most sophisticated technologies of all time. Without the dedication of powerful resources and the use of advanced techniques, it is practically impossible to backtrack and trace someone's identity (*Mirea et al., 2018*). The following diagram shows how traffic flows through the TOR network (*Zhang, 2019*):

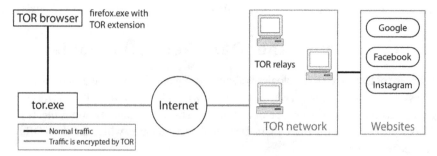

Figure 2.2 – Traffic flow when using the TOR network

Because browser plugins can be tricked into disclosing your IP address, browser plugins such as Flash, RealPlayer, QuickTime, and others are blocked by the TOR browser. Despite its advanced capabilities and features, a TOR browser deployment is a relatively straightforward process that requires no advanced knowledge, and it does not differ from traditional browser installations. It is compatible with all major computer and mobile operating systems—that is, Windows, Linux, macOS, Android, and iOS. With at least three layers of encryption, onion routing re-routes communication across a network of relays, much like the layers of an onion. Throughout this process, it masks the user's original IP address, making the connection highly anonymous and secure (*Porup, 2019*).

The TOR network consists of four main components (*Carnielli, Aiash,* and *Alazab, 2021*):

- **The TOR client**: This is software installed on the device of a TOR user. This software creates a circuit that is anonymous and handles all cryptographic keys needed to communicate with all the necessary servers within the circuit.

- **Entry/guard node**: This is the circuit's first relay and it receives the client request and sends it to the next node in the TOR network.

- **Middle nodes**: Middle nodes are neither a guard nor an exit, but act as the connection between the two.

- **Exit node**: This is the circuit's last relay.

The following figure shows how traffic flows when using the TOR network:

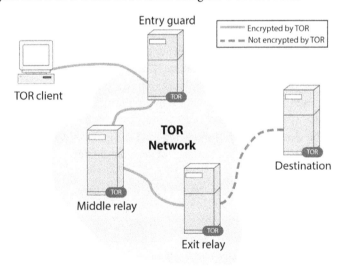

Figure 2.3 – The TOR network

The link between the entrance and exit relays is encrypted, as seen in *Figure 2.3*. The **Advanced Encryption Standard** (**AES**) is used to accomplish this. However, there is no encryption used for the communication between the exit node and the ultimate destination. This suggests that an attacker waiting nearby the destination will be able to see data packets if the connection between the client and the final destination is not encrypted as part of a higher security protocol, such as HTTPS (*Carnielli, Aiash*, and *Alazab, 2021*). The popular Google Chrome browser and the TOR browser are compared in the following table (*Slant, 2021*):

Google Chrome	TOR browser
Syncs between devices	Extremely slow
Plenty of extensions	Access hidden onion sites
Simple user interface	Free and open source
Online tracking by default	Safe and private browsing
A big target for hackers	Dependent on Mozilla Firefox
Huge memory hog	Too many reCAPTCHAs on sites

Figure 2.4 – Google Chrome versus TOR browser

The use of TOR and other anonymous browsers is not illegal. In fact, such dark browsers can be used to privately access both the public internet and deeper parts of the web. The privacy offered by the TOR network is significant in the current digital era. Corporations, organizations, and governing bodies participate in mass unauthorized surveillance of users' online activity. Some people do not want the government or even ISPs to monitor their web browsing. Users in authoritarian regimes are often prevented from accessing some parts of the internet. The combination of TOR and a VPN can help these users access blocked content without being tracked (*Jardine, 2015*). The following section describes how the TOR network can be utilized in mobile technologies.

Orbot – the mobile version of the TOR browser

Orbot is a free app that provides anonymity for Android users. This app is integrated with TOR and allows traffic to route through several nodes on the TOR network. The TOR project team stated that Orbot has a built-in VPN feature that helps users bypass firewalls and access blocked content. Orbot ensures that users' data and privacy remain protected from the prying eyes of the government and ISPs (*Ajaay, 2019*).

Orbot's user interface is straightforward to learn, and users do not have to configure anything for basic use. However, a more advanced configuration is also available for experienced users, allowing them to configure Orbot as they prefer. The Orbot app is available on Android devices via the Google Play

Store. Presently, users cannot download Orbot on a computer unless they use an Android emulator (*Wishapplist, 2021*). The following list describes some of Orbot's most significant advantages (*Ajaay, 2019*):

- **Ad-free and open source**: Unlike traditional VPN apps that promote ads whenever the apps are opened or used, Orbot is free of ads. This is because Orbot is open source, and anyone can check the code of the software.

- **Protection against network surveillance**: Orbot encrypts users' traffic, and the data packets travel through several nodes before reaching the end server. In this way, the app ensures that users' data remains protected from hackers, law enforcement agencies, and the government.

- **Root access**: Users can proxy (route) all of their outgoing traffic from their Android device through Orbot if they have root/administrative access. Users can also manage which apps they want to use with Orbot.

This specialized app is one of the most challenging and advanced mediums adopted by cybercriminals all over the world. You can use the app to make other apps on your Android device run through its encrypted tunnel. The following screenshot shows what Orbot's basic interface looks like on Android phones (*Raue, 2022*):

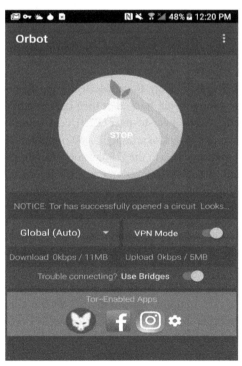

Figure 2.5 – Orbot's basic interface

Apps for Android and iOS are continuously collecting and selling your personal information, keeping it on unsecured servers, and monitoring everything you do online. Thankfully, you may regain your privacy by using Orbot and a strong VPN to send your data through the encrypted TOR network. This prevents the apps themselves, marketing firms, or other third parties from viewing or making money off of your apps, texts, or other actions.

Conclusion to the TOR network

The TOR browser takes privacy to new extremes. However, there are restrictions on how anonymous the TOR browser is when it comes to disguising your browsing activity and location. Your ISP can still tell that you're using TOR even though it can't access your browsing history or the data that TOR has encrypted. What has been discussed so far constitutes only a part of the complex mechanisms and advanced procedures taking place in the TOR network. There are specific key characteristics that substantially affect TOR's workflow. Users of the TOR browser can customize the browser's performance and anonymity to suit their individual needs. For instance, users who value their anonymity greatly (such as dissidents) might prefer their traffic flow uniformly across all routers to reduce the possibility of their traffic being compromised by high-bandwidth routers. On the other hand, users who are less concerned with privacy and only utilize the network for casual online browsing may place a higher emphasis on performance and feel more at ease utilizing high-bandwidth routers (*Snader* and *Borisov*, *2008*).

I2P

I2P is another widely used Dark Web technology. Every day, people use this complex software to connect with the world without worrying about being tracked or their data being collected by others. I2P is a privacy-focus networking tool that allows **peer-to-peer** (**P2P**), censorship-resistant communications. Its traffic passes through a volunteer network of around 55,000 computers that are distributed around the world. All I2P traffic is internal and stays in the I2P network. Additionally, traffic inside I2P does not directly interact with the internet, as it is a layer on top of the internet. No one can see where the traffic is going, where it is coming from, or what the contents of the data packets are (*Khosrow-Pour*, *2020*). At the moment, there are more than 30,000 I2P users worldwide.

As with TOR, users can host hidden sites, called *eepsites* (for I2P). These kinds of sites have a `.i2p` domain extension and typically require I2P to connect too (although people hosting `.i2p` sites can allow their sites to be viewed by non-I2P users). By using a network of proxy servers, the I2P technology's routing protocol constructs difficult-to-trace communication routes. With this protocol, the proxy servers receive messages from numerous senders, shuffle them, and then deliver them back to the next recipient in random order. By severing the connection between the request's source and its destination, this method makes it more difficult for hackers and eavesdroppers to track **end-to-end** (**E2E**) conversations. This type of protocol offers good security even if a hacker can see the full path, although it is not flawless. The transmitter and recipient of the data packets can be tracked by adversaries using sophisticated correlation techniques (*Egger, Schlumberger, Kruegel,* and *Vigna, 2013*). The following list describes some of I2P's main disadvantages (*Black, 2021*):

- **Complex installation and usage**: It necessitates a drawn-out installation procedure and specific browser settings.

- **Mandatory logging**: The I2P user interface must be logged in for users to access their material.

- **Potential vulnerabilities**: Thousands of users were exposed to a zero-day vulnerability that I2P experienced in 2014. Later, a 2017 study found that several more I2P flaws were also exploited.

- **A smaller user base than TOR**: I2P is substantially more vulnerable to attacks as a result of having fewer network nodes and servers.

- **Less anonymity when browsing indexed sites**: When users surf indexed sites, I2P does not promise complete anonymity. This issue might be resolved by using VPN services.

It turns out that using I2P for accessing the Dark Web has significant benefits and thought-provoking drawbacks. It is recommended to choose I2P for total security when you are using instant messages, web pages, and torrent downloads. Just be aware that the user base is still relatively small and bad threat actors have not had the time to break in yet. Also, be aware that you—and your electronic device—will be connected with other people seeking anonymity. You may be sharing tunnel communications with people you do not want to share with.

Freenet

The Freenet concept was originally developed by Ian Clarke, but it has been undergoing constant development since the year 2000. Freenet is an **open source software (OSS)** that is used for accessing the Dark Web. It is used for P2P communications over the internet while providing high anonymity and security. Freenet works on a decentralized network and is designed in such a way that allows freedom of speech without censorship (*Levine et al., 2020*).

The Freenet technology is different from conventional P2P sharing software in terms of both its interactivity and security features. *Freenet can be used only for accessing digital content that was uploaded to the Freenet network.* In general, Freenet is used for distributing content, downloading files, publishing *freesites*, communicating through message boards, and activating forums. Communication on Freenet is routed through alternate nodes, which dramatically decreases the chance that users will be traced. Here are some of the main disadvantages of Freenet (*Kalyani, 2021*):

- The users have no knowledge of which files their nodes store

- Each node has a limited storage capacity

- No user knows the identity of a server that provides a file they have requested

- Users do not know the identity of a node that has requested a file from them

The Freenet technology enables users to anonymously distribute information by sharing bandwidth and hard drive space. By distributing short, encrypted chunks of content across its users' computers and connecting solely through intermediary machines that transmit requests for content and deliver them back without knowing the complete contents of the file, Freenet can offer anonymity on the internet. Freenet is usually defined as an internet within the internet because people are not limited to sharing files, but may use it for any purpose.

The use of cryptocurrencies on the Dark Web

An anonymous digital currency has been a concept since at least 2008. The domain name `bitcoin.org` was registered on August 18, 2008. An article titled *Bitcoin: A Peer-to-Peer Electronic Cash System* appeared later that year, on October 31, posted to a cryptography mailing list. A P2P network can be used to construct a system for electronic transactions without depending on a central authority, according to a paper written by a person using the supposed pseudonym *Satoshi Nakamoto*. The first Bitcoins were mined by Nakamoto on January 3, 2009, giving rise to the **Bitcoin** (**BTC**) technology (*Bernard* and *Kay*, *2021*).

Introduction to cryptocurrencies

One of the most lasting mysteries of Bitcoin is the real identity of its founder. Over the years, several people have said that it is Satoshi Nakamoto. Bitcoin's founder remains unknown until this day, and little is known about him. It is believed that his last email communication was in April 2011. As of November 2021, Nakamoto was considered one of the wealthiest persons in the world, with an estimated net worth of 73 billion US dollars. His crypto holdings are approximately between 750,000 to 1.1 million BTC (*Cuthbertson*, *2021*). The following screenshot shows some of cryptocurrencies' basic features (*PwC*, *2021*):

Cryptocurrency

Cryptocurrencies are a way to create, exchange, and store money in the blockchain. By using cryptographic mechanisms users are able to verify the transfer of funds.

Has no intrinsic value as it is not redeemable for other commodities such as gold.

It exists only in the blockchain and it has no physical form.

Its supply is not controlled by a central bank and the network is 100% decentralized.

Figure 2.6 – Cryptocurrencies' basic features

A cryptocurrency (crypto) is a virtual currency that is secured by cryptographic mechanisms. Its decentralized nature makes it *almost impossible* to *counterfeit or double-spend*. Cryptocurrencies are based on advanced *Blockchain technology*, which is a system that records data in a way that is almost impossible to change, hack, or cheat the system (*Berentsen* and *Schär, 2018*). The following screenshot shows how Blockchain works (*PwC, 2021*):

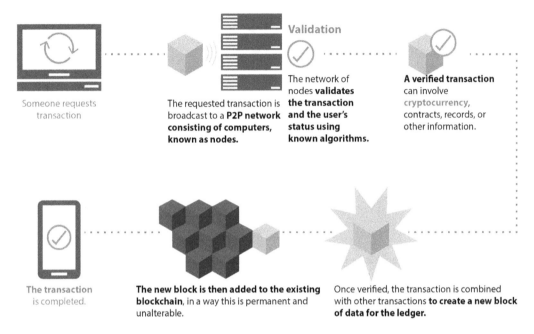

Figure 2.7 – How Blockchain works

The core idea behind cryptocurrencies was to create a secure, fast, reliable, and anonymous way to transfer monetary value from one person to another. Since Bitcoin's release in 2009, its value has skyrocketed, and recently, it has been labeled by its users as the new *digital gold*. At some point, Bitcoin's market cap exceeded 1 trillion US dollars, and millions of people worldwide trade this currency daily (*Kharpal, 2021*). In 2011, rival cryptocurrencies started to appear, with Namecoin, Litecoin, and Swiftcoin all making their debut (*Cavendish, 2021*). Nowadays, there are thousands of cryptocurrencies in existence, with the most popular being Bitcoin and Ethereum. The following screenshot shows the number of cryptocurrencies globally from 2013 to October 2021 (*Statista, 2021*):

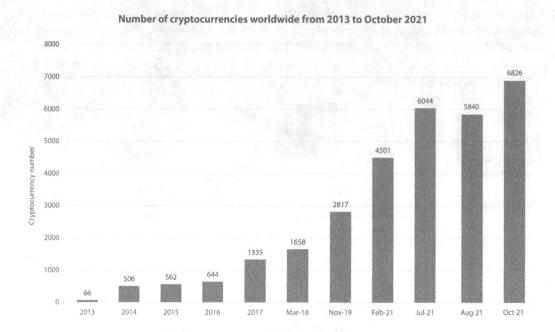

Figure 2.8 – Cryptocurrencies' growth over the years

There are various platforms where anyone can buy all kinds of cryptocurrencies. To name a few: Binance, Coinbase, Crypto.com, Kraken, and many others. If you are a newbie to the crypto world, figuring out how to buy the various available cryptocurrencies can be confusing at first. Thankfully, learning the basics of cryptocurrency investing is not too difficult. By following these five simple steps, you can begin investing in cryptocurrencies:

1. **Choose a broker or crypto exchange**: The first step to buying a cryptocurrency is to choose from the thousands of crypto exchanges and brokers that are available in the market. Both ways offer significant advantages, and they are relatively safe approaches to trading cryptocurrencies with ease and convenience.

2. **Create and verify your account**: The second step is to sign up in order to open an account. Depending on the amount and platform you want to buy, you may have to verify your identity. This is an essential step in the signing-up process and helps to prevent fraud and comply with anti-money-laundering regulatory requirements and procedures.

3. **Deposit funds to invest**: To buy cryptocurrencies, you need to make sure that you have cash in your account. There are various ways you can do this: credit/debit cards, PayPal accounts, bank transfers, single-use virtual cards, and many others. Depending on your funding method, you may have to wait a few days before you can use the money you deposit.

4. **Place your cryptocurrency order**: Now, you are ready to place your first order. There are thousands of cryptocurrencies to choose from, ranging from the most famous such as Bitcoin, Ethereum, and Tether to more obscure cryptos such as Theta, Fuel, and Holo. With most brokers and exchanges, you can buy fractional shares of cryptocurrency.

5. **Select a storage method**: Cryptocurrency platforms are not backed by institutions such as the UK's **Financial Services Compensation Scheme (FSCS)**. These platforms are at risk of hacking or theft, and you could even lose your funds if you forget the credentials to access your account. That's why it's of vital importance to have a secure storage place for your cryptocurrencies. Here are some ways to achieve this:

    *   **Leave the crypto on the exchange**: The crypto you buy is usually stored in a so-called crypto wallet. If you don't like the exchange, you might transfer it off the platform to a separate hot or cold wallet. Depending on the exchange and the amount you transfer, you may be obliged to pay a small fee to do this.

    *   **Hot wallets**: These are wallets that exist on the internet and run on digital-connected devices, such as computers, phones, or tablets. Hot wallets are pretty secure and convenient, but there's some risk of theft since they're connected to the internet.

    *   **Cold wallets**: These kinds of wallets take the form of external devices, such as a USB drive or a hard drive. They are not connected to the internet, thereby protecting the wallet from unauthorized access. You have to be very careful with cold wallets—for example, if you lose the words/passwords associated with them, you may permanently lose access to your crypto funds.

To play the game, one must respect cryptocurrencies while realizing that they are a high-risk investment. Because of the asset's volatility, extended periods of rising valuation cannot be ruled out in the future, even though crashes do happen. Additionally, many people find value in the aspirational symbolism of a decentralized, yet realized, digital future, which makes cryptocurrencies deserving of careful study. However, there are still ethical concerns surrounding cryptocurrencies, so until they are straightened out, I'd approach the venture with caution.

The use of cryptocurrencies on the Dark Web

Of all of Bitcoin's uses—for example, as a currency, a payment method, a commodity, a technology, a market hedge, and so on—probably its most notorious use is as a facilitator of online illegal transactions. In Bitcoin's early years, the currency quickly emerged as the primary payment method of choice for illicit activities, including human trafficking and child pornography (*Christopher, 2014*). Throughout the years, Bitcoin has allowed anonymous Dark Web transactions on eBay-like markets, avoiding the use of conventional currencies and thus the easy intervention of law enforcement (*Lowrey, 2021*).

Specifically, one of the first Dark Web drug markets, *Silk Road*, relied heavily on Bitcoin. Thanks to Bitcoin's unregulated and borderless payment system, Silk Road became a key player on the Dark Web. The founder of Silk Road, *Ross Ulbricht*, had successfully created a platform where it was easy for everybody to buy all kinds of products from the comfort of their home (*Christin, 2013*). The anonymity offered by Bitcoin made Silk Road highly attractive to both sellers and buyers. Bitcoin's anonymity, along with the cryptographic mechanisms of TOR, has led to an explosion of crime facilitated via the internet (*Kumar* and *Rosenbach, 2019*).

In 2013, after months of investigating the Silk Road community, the FBI eventually managed to take down Silk Road and arrest Ulbricht in the San Francisco Library (US). The FBI agents took Ulbricht's laptop and collected all damning evidence. After the arrest of Ulbricht, more than *1 billion US dollars' worth of Bitcoins* were seized and kept in a secret place. Since that incident, critics have brought up the illicit use of Bitcoin on the Dark Web as an argument against the push for widespread acceptance (*Greenberg, 2020*). The following screenshot shows what the Silk Road website looked like after its seizure by the FBI (*BBC News, 2013*):

THIS HIDDEN SITE HAS BEEN SEIZED

by the Federal Bureau of Investigation,
in conjunction with the IRS Criminal Investigation Division,
ICE Homeland Security Investigations, and the Drug Enforcement Administration,
in accordance with a seizure warrant obtained by the
United States Attorney's Office for the Southern District of New York
and issued pursuant to 18 U.S.C. § 983(j) by the
United States District Court for the Southern District of New York

Figure 2.8 – Silk Road's seizure by the FBI

On the other hand, Bitcoin's anonymity has been, in many cases, a massive help for police investigations. In this regard, a transaction between a crypto exchange and a bank account may reveal a range of interlinked illegal activities, including drug trafficking. During the last decade, more private banks, financial intelligence units, regulators, and investigators have been working collaboratively to uncover the patterns criminal groups use to monetize crime operations (*Monroe, 2020*). Furthermore, Interpol (France) and the Bavarian State Ministry of Justice (Germany) created the Working Group on Darknet and Cryptocurrencies. The purpose of this group was to do the following (*Interpol, 2021*):

- Share tools and methodologies for finding criminals who use cryptocurrencies on the Dark Web
- Discuss online investigations' best practices
- Establish forensic solutions and investigative standards for law enforcement

To address the most critical challenges, the group set up the Dark Web and Cryptocurrencies Task Force with the aim of doing the following (*Interpol, 2021*):

- Establishing a worldwide database of criminal cryptocurrency wallets

- Standardizing the language used to categorize the data gathered or *crawled* from the Dark Web

- Creating a community of innovative minds and software developers from law enforcement to lead these efforts

Conclusion to cryptocurrencies

Without a doubt, cryptocurrencies have brought many benefits (that is, privacy and anonymity) and have the potential to enable financial and social growth in many societies, including developing countries. However, protecting privacy advocates should not come at the expense of empowering human traffickers, child abusers, and drug lords. Therein lies the challenge for law enforcement and regulators: to devise approaches that walk the fine line of safeguarding liberal principles in an age of information control and, at the same time, identifying and eradicating the most heinous crimes on the Dark Web. For this reason, tackling crypto-related crimes requires cooperation between the government, law enforcement, the private sector, civil society, the community, and academia.

Summary

A variety of subjects were covered in this chapter. Discovering the node path and layer-by-layer data encryption is almost difficult due to the intricate processes used by Dark Web technologies. Websites are unable to trace the geolocation and IP of their users, and users are unable to obtain this information about the host site due to the exceptionally high level of encryption and security. With the usage of cryptocurrencies, users' Darknet communication becomes highly secure, enabling users to communicate, see plenty of material, and share files in confidence. The next chapter makes an introduction to the major crimes that take place on the Dark Web. Specifically, it covers drug markets and how criminals disseminate illegal substances by using the Dark Web.

Part 2:
The Dark Web's Ecosystem and Major Crimes

Even though accessing the Dark Web is lawful, much of what happens there is criminal. Through encryption, users of dark websites can maintain their anonymity. Anyone involved in crime will find this appealing. Additionally, it is helpful for whistleblowers who worry about retaliation and political dissidents who live in totalitarian regimes. It is therefore legal to use the Dark Web, but it also gives access to unlawful activities and contraband. Part 2 aims to allow the reader to understand the Dark Web's ecosystem (both the good and bad sides) as well as the major crimes that occur on this hidden part of the internet.

This part has the following chapters:

- *Chapter 3, Drug Markets on the Dark Web*
- *Chapter 4, Child Pornography on the Dark Web*
- *Chapter 5, Human Trafficking on the Dark Web*
- *Chapter 6, Cyberterrorism on the Dark Web*

3
Drug Markets on the Dark Web

The everyday use of the World Wide Web has allowed an easy engagement with various global services. For example, **electronic commerce** (**e-commerce**) is a highly developing sector with an estimated 2.3 trillion US dollars in worldwide sales per year. In spite of the countless legal tangible products and services offered by vendors and manufacturers, illegal platforms have also expanded online. The most worrying for international authorities is the Dark Web, and specifically the markets that exist on this hidden part of the internet. Dark markets (also known as DNMs) are commercial websites on the Dark Web that work via networks such as TOR, I2P, and Freenet. Precisely, the Dark Web consists of markets that have to do with drugs, human trafficking, firearms, child sexual abuse material, assassinations, cyber-arms, counterfeit products, and other disturbing activities. In the last few years, law enforcement authorities and police agents have put massive efforts to fight commercial Dark Web marketplaces (*Liggett et al., 2020*).

The manufacture and sale of illicit drugs remain two of the oldest and highest-grossing illegal industries. Just as e-commerce has changed the way we conduct business and buy services, so has the internet drastically impacted the 21st-century landscape of drug distribution. Drug sellers and buyers see the Dark Web as a lucrative safe haven. Almost a decade after the demise of Silk Road, the world's largest-ever drug marketplace, the Dark Web is still the main avenue for trading illicit drugs. Imagine online drug markets allowing you to order an ounce of marijuana or a kilo of cocaine with the same comfort as buying books on Amazon. In many cases, those involved in Dark Web drug trading are able to quickly adapt and adjust their strategies to decrease the chances of detection and prosecution. The operation of international law enforcement and the underlying legal frameworks within which these organizations function face a serious challenge from this new type of retail market. This chapter will cover the following topics:

- Drug markets' ecosystem
- What enables transactions between buyers and sellers
- Ways law enforcement, the private sector, and the public fight Dark Web drug markets
- The impact of the Dark Web on drug trafficking

Drug markets' ecosystem

The increasingly sophisticated, user-friendly, and impersonal global network of drug markets make the illegal drug trade a dynamic area that is subject to fast changes, with marketplaces appearing and disappearing on a regular basis. These drug markets host hundreds—or, in some cases, thousands—of individuals who sell drugs, commonly known as *vendors*. The Dark Web offers significant anonymity for both vendors and buyers, who use digital currencies such as Bitcoin to process transactions.

The first drug transaction on the internet is believed that it took place during the 1970s. According to reports, it involved students who exchanged cannabis at the **Massachusetts Institute of Technology (MIT)** and Stanford University. Since that year, drugs have been sold digitally in both small and large volumes. In the late 1990s, discussion forums and groups, related to the manufacture and use of drugs, have also appeared online. One of the most widely known drug forums, called *The Hive*, was launched in 1997, with the purpose of sharing information related to practical drug synthesis. Participants in this forum ranged from self-declared organized crime chemists to pure theorists, as well as forensic chemists. As the following screenshot shows, Dark Web drug markets appear to be dominated by vendors from the US, Australia, and the United Kingdom (*EMCDDA, 2017*):

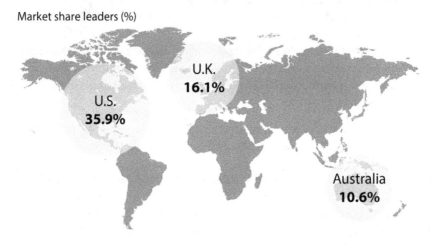

Figure 3.1 – Dominant drug vendors on the Dark Web

As of today, Dark Web drug sale amounts to 315 million dollars annually, up from 80 million dollars per year just in 2017. In 2015, a leading academic expert in the UK, called Gareth Owenson, reported that 15.4 percent of the Dark Web's indexed websites were related to drugs. All online platforms, including illegal ones, operate in order to make the exchange of goods and services more convenient. Therefore, platforms will expand and grow if they offer significant benefits to both sellers and buyers. The illegal drugs sold on Dark Web markets are predominantly cannabis, stimulants (cocaine, amphetamines), and ecstasy-type drugs. The drug trade has become increasingly profitable because of the global network of traffickers and dealers who offer customers ease of availability, convenience, and level of choice. After discovering a drug market, the potential user has to sign up, usually with a referral link, after which they can see the various products. A further password may be needed to perform transactions. These practices better protect users against login credential compromise and facilitate a unique experience of freedom within a libertarian framework (*Long, 2022*).

The most common drugs sold in drug markets are often those used recreationally or for parties (cannabis, ecstasy, MDMA, and so on). The contrasts between *online* and *offline* markets may be explained by the fact that purchases made on online drug markets often need some forethought, which may not be appropriate for everyday use by heroin addicts, for example. The chance of detection is also an essential factor when it comes to Dark Web drug markets. It is obvious that sellers and buyers will be keen to follow markets that have relatively low chances of identification. The combination of TOR, public key algorithms, and cryptocurrencies indeed make the chance of detection very low. There is not much evidence, but as shown in the following screenshot both drug buyers and sellers seem to be young, educated, entrepreneurial males from Western Europe or English-speaking countries:

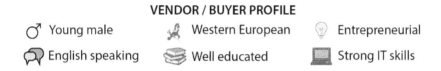

VENDOR / BUYER PROFILE

♂ Young male   Western European   Entrepreneurial

English speaking   Well educated   Strong IT skills

Figure 3.2 – Profile of drug markets vendors and buyers

The use of the Dark Web to promote illegal drug activities is coming under more and more pressure from the authorities. According to a BBC report from 2020, 500 kg of illegal drugs were seized after a coordinated international raid by police forces on Dark Web drug markets. Four Britons were detained as a result of the raids. If you are found guilty of taking, carrying, producing, or distributing (also known as supplying) illegal substances, you could receive a fine or a prison sentence. The sort of drug, the quantity in your possession, and whether you were involved in its production or supply will all affect how severely you will be punished (*Tidy, 2020*).

In the last decades, drug markets have started shifting to the digital world, and they can be mainly found on the Dark Web. Transitioning from offline to digital drug markets affects how vendors sell and disseminate drugs (*Aldridge* and *Décary-Hétu, 2016*). Drug vendors can now communicate with customers over the Dark Web and provide illegal drugs without the need to meet the customer. On most drug websites, administrators utilize e-commerce systems/methods to push equal practices between vendors, as well as to indicate to buyers which vendors are most legit and trustworthy. Specifically, these systems use conventional techniques such as the following (*Liggett et al., 2021*):

- Ranking vendors on the site

- Displaying the number of successful transactions a vendor has done

- Showing the shipment quality

- Providing a rating between one and five stars

The following screenshot shows a review page from **Silk Road**, one of the biggest and most sophisticated online drug markets of all time (*VICE, 2022*):

Rating	review	freshness
5 of 5	Quick shipping, beautiful product, decent stealth. weighed out to 991mg, which is within the realm of error.	1 day
5 of 5	will update when tested/tasted but no reason to suspect with all the positive reviews.	1 day
5 of 5	Fast Shipping, great packaging	1 day
5 of 5	10/5 fast arrived in 4 days – double vacum sealed in stealth packaging. looks on spot – smells like licorice and very very clean!	1 day
5 of 5	A+ service. Excellent communication and delivery. Will update if product is anything but excellent.	1 day
5 of 5	Excellent service and shipping! Thank you very much. YESSSS!!! ORDER FROM THIS VENDOR!! This ketamine is amazing. Packaging/stealth was dead on 5/5 A+++. Even if the package was opened there's little chance that anyone would be messing with the contents.	1 day
5 of 5	Now as the the actual package's contents... 5/5!! It's the largest crystals Ive ever seen in a K package before. I crushed the smallest amount yesterday and was feeling great. I can't wait to have a full blown experience on this extraordinarily clean product. HIGHLY RECOMMENDED VENDOR!!	2 days
5 of 5	Just in time for the weekend :) Wish I could give 6/5. Seller went above and beyond what a retail store would. Answered questions promptly,	2 days
5 of 5	shipped within 24 hours, recieved 3 days from time of order. Excellent stealth! Product was just as described receieved in one shard :) Will be ordering again.	2 days

Figure 3.3 – Review page of Silk Road (accessed 25 November 2013)

It's arguable that the professionalism of the customer service provided by this infamous marketplace and the fact that clients felt safe and at ease purchasing there contributed to its popularity. Illegal trade on Dark Web markets is a demonstration of the complicated nature of mutative organized crime. Dark Web markets, also known as crypto markets, provide a highly secure way for buying illicit drugs, services, and goods. Almost any kind of drug is available to buyers with relative ease, including psychoactive substances. Most customers appear to be drug users who use drugs occasionally or have used drugs in the past. They are drawn to crypto markets because they are thought to offer increased safety, better quality, and variety, as well as convenience and speed of delivery. Buyers like to base their purchases on the following:

- Price
- Details of products
- Available trip reports (description of personal experiences with the effects of specific substances)
- Vendor reputation
- Feedback from other buyers

Furthermore, another important aspect of the Dark Web drug market is that each drug website lists the categories of illegal drugs in different ways. Typically, this happens by the category of the drug, such as opioids or stimulants, though categorization may not be standard. An example is a category with pills. In this category, other relevant drug types such as benzodiazepines may be listed. Additionally, there are examples where categories have been purposefully misdeclared to promote them to buyers of other drugs. Compared to their prevalence on the Surface Web, new psychoactive substances seem to play a little role in the drug market arena on the Dark Web.

What enables transactions between buyers and sellers

Anonymization services, such as TOR, enable users to hide, meaning that they can browse the internet without revealing their personal identification details. Additionally, specific services allow websites to be anonymously hosted by hiding the servers' location—a feature known as *hidden services*. Because of these characteristics, dark markets can sell illegal products in an open fashion, providing a highly anonymous comfort to their users. While anonymization services have largely been recognized for illegal, often criminal reasons, their original purpose was different. There are many permissible and legal purposes for which citizens may wish to use these hidden services—for example, news leaks, whistleblowing, anonymous browsing, and many others.

In the last few years, there has been a dramatic expansion in the sale of various illegal substances on the Dark Web drug markets, with online sales estimated to increase exponentially due to expanding evolving technologies and the wide use of mobile technologies. Discussion forums and chat rooms enable sharing information on the safety of drugs, as well as optimal dosing use that reduces the risk of serious illness or harm. These discussion forums and chat rooms create a community of people in a non-judgmental environment where users feel comfortable with each other. There doesn't seem to be a particular list of staff members and their corresponding positions for Dark Web forums. However, forum moderators have a *Super Moderator Title* mark on their profile cover while administrators have a *Verified Members* mark, making both staff jobs obvious (*Digital Shadows, 2020*).

Dark Web drug users and sellers alike can freely express themselves in ways that are not seen in real life. Specifically, a user of the Silk Road platform highlights the benefits of the site: "*The community here is awesome. I mean look in the forums, there is a "Drug Safety" forum. The whole philosophy behind the place is that if you want to put heroin in your body, go ahead. But hey, if you want to get off that nasty drug, we're here to help you too. It's not like real life where street dealers might coerce you into keeping your addiction or whatever*" (*Buxton and Bingham, 2015*).

Another Silk Road user stated: "*MUCH safer, you know what you're getting, you can see reviews of the product before you buy. The feedback system is revolutionary for a market like this. All my fears about quality are gone. I know what I'm getting and I know that it's good. Security of the transaction, less chance of violence, the rating and feedback system gives some confidence on the quality and substance. Mostly I buy by vendor reputation and buyer reports from the forums*" (*Buxton and Bingham, 2015*).

To enable transactions between a seller and a buyer without either being traceable, there are five significant conditions to be met (*EMCDDA, 2017*):

- **Privacy**: The people who participate in the transaction must communicate without any risk of their connection being intercepted. In conventional mail services, people communicate by placing material in sealed envelopes. In digital communications, participants use cryptography—for example, public-key cryptography, also known as asymmetric encryption. This makes it almost impossible to decrypt without using the private key.

- **Anonymity**: The senders' and recipients' identities must be concealed in order for the communication to be protected from outsiders. In the instance of conventional postal services, the same applies to the senders—for example, to not put their address or name on the cover of the envelope. For Dark Web communications, the TOR network allows this through onion-routing mechanisms, anonymous accounts, and unidentifiable email addresses.

- **Authentication**: Each part of the communication must be 100 percent sure that the connection is truly coming from the person who claims to be the sender and recipient; the same applies to a traditional mail letter, with a signature that was handwritten. Authentication mechanisms are also featured in the most secure communication technologies and software.

- **Hidden exchange**: For achieving reliable and secure transactions, vendors need to have the ability to run their market without the chance of being exposed. Offline, this is possible for vendors who operate without permanent premises or licenses. In Dark Web environments, hidden services that are offered in hidden networks—such as the TOR browser—allow vendors to run their online markets without the chance of detection or prosecution.

- **Payment**: For a transaction conducted through the Dark Web, it is essential that the transaction cannot be identified as occurred by the buyer. In real life, this is guaranteed by paying in cash. Anonymizing hidden services allow sellers, buyers, and vendors to communicate without revealing their **personal identifiable information** (**PII**). However, in order to achieve complete anonymity, the transaction must also be carried out anonymously. In digital Dark Web transactions, cryptocurrencies are used.

Many Dark Web drug markets have started using a more advanced layer of security in order to offer more reliable transactions. This is known as an **escrow service**. In a simple escrow system, when a user buys an item, the fee is temporarily held by a third party. The fee is given to the seller only after the buyer has clarified and confirmed that they have received the product or service. More sophisticated escrow methods use **multi-signature** (or **multi-sig**) confirmation transactions. This implies that two out of the three parties involved—the buyer, the seller, and the market—must confirm the transaction, rather than merely the buyer confirming that the order was successful. While multi-sig escrow services may be available in the majority of drug marketplaces, they are not necessarily the best option.

Drugs purchased via dark markets are usually shipped to consumers through postal services (though not always to the customer's front door). When providing shipping details, it is a common practice for customers to give an address different than their actual house of residence—for example, a neighbor's residence, a vacant house, a business building, or a post box (*Martin, 2014*). This happens to reduce the chance of identification in case the police find the package and its content. Even if the police manage to identify an illegal drug package, there are difficulties in obtaining sufficient evidence for prosecution.

Dark Web discussion forums offer detailed guidance on how to avoid the attention of postal services and law enforcement (*Boffey, 2019*). When using a drug market website, buyers are advised to use pseudonyms and unidentifiable forms of payment—for example, cryptocurrencies, single-use credit cards, electronic wallets, and others. Additionally, those who ship illegal substances are counseled to send goods in quantities that will result in the lightest penalties. If detected, the seller's sentence will probably be small and understate the gravity of the crimes committed. The following list indicates the characteristics that online dark marketplaces usually have (*Liggett et al., 2021*):

- Dependence on Dark Web networks, such as TOR and I2P

- Third-party administration, management, and hosting

- Utilization of cryptonyms to conceal users' identities

- Use of traditional mail services to deliver products

- Use of website moderators to increase trust among sellers and buyers

- Decentralized advanced networks

- Use of cryptographic digital currencies

Furthermore, several Dark Web drug sites pretend to be legitimate shops or some kind of marketplace with the purpose of defrauding people. At any point, a centralized market escrow has the ability to close down and leave with the buyers' and vendors' cryptocurrencies. This has occurred in multiple instances, such as with the *Evolution*, *Wall Street Market*, and *BlackBank* platforms. In addition, some websites frequently reach a point of good reputation maturity when they have sold enough products and have amassed a sizable number of escrowed cryptocurrencies; many decide to quit with the money rather than compete at the higher-priced, bigger-volume matured product level.

Ways law enforcement, the private sector, and the public fight Dark Web drug markets

The development and accessibility of anonymization tools, the emergence of a new tech-savvy generation, the development and accessibility of hidden drug markets, the evolution of cryptocurrencies, and—most importantly—the continued global demand for illicit drugs are all expected to contribute to the exponential growth of drug markets. The value of Dark Web drug marketplaces and the incentives to engage in supply are factors why drug markets will continue to expand. Efforts to create alternative, *risk-free* (or low-risk) transaction chains will continue to be driven by the criminalization of the trade. This section highlights the major approaches that are being used by law enforcement, the private sector, and the community to identify and stop drug trafficking on the Dark Web:

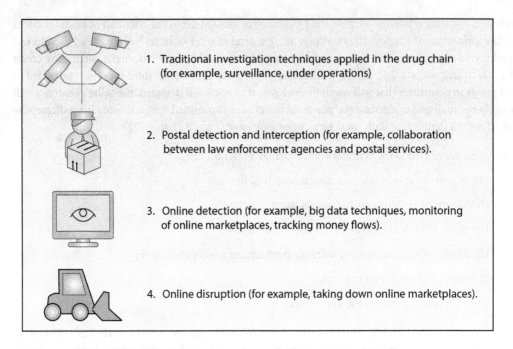

1. Traditional investigation techniques applied in the drug chain (for example, surveillance, under operations)

2. Postal detection and interception (for example, collaboration between law enforcement agencies and postal services).

3. Online detection (for example, big data techniques, monitoring of online marketplaces, tracking money flows).

4. Online disruption (for example, taking down online marketplaces).

Figure 3.4 – Modes of detection and intervention

Drug activity conducted on the Dark Web is a natural result of the anonymity that special browsers grant to users—for example, TOR and I2P. In order to combat drug trafficking on the Dark Web, jurisdictional laws and shared data need to be more fluid. This can be done by sharing evidence with other relevant organizations for the end goal of bringing drug lords to justice. Although there are various methods of combating drug markets on the Dark Web, they all have flaws to some extent, including advanced law enforcement tools.

Some people believe that the only proper solution to the drug trafficking problem would be to get rid of the Dark Web altogether. However, due to its benefits, as well as its technical complexities, *the Dark Web cannot be shut down completely (Smith, 2016)*. Acknowledging that there is no possible way to eliminate the Dark Web in its entirety, it is significant to move forward knowing that the impact of Dark Web drug trafficking can be mitigated. We'll now examine the existing methods that law enforcement and the private sector use to fight this kind of crime:

BITCRIME

Digital cryptographic currencies are pseudo-anonymous and traded directly between users in **peer-to-peer (P2P)** networks. This kind of currency makes traditional ways of regulation and law enforcement reach their limits. BITCRIME was a German-Austrian project that had to do with the prevention and prosecution of organized financial crimes committed with virtual currencies, including Dark Web drug trafficking. The project was funded by the **Austrian Federal Ministry for Transport, Innovation,**

and Technology (BMVIT) and the **German Federal Ministry of Education and Research (BMBF)**. The project's duration was 28 months (October 2014-January 2017), and it cost approximately 2.4 million euros (*BITCRIME, 2021*).

BITCRIME's aim was the development of practical and innovative approaches to identify, prosecute, and prevent crimes with digital currencies. Over a period of 2 years, organizational and technical approaches were developed to enable effective criminal investigations while, at the same time, avoiding a blanket ban on digital currencies and potential misuse through mass surveillance. Essential requirements to be met were financial efficiency for BITCRIME's involved parties and a judicious balance between economic potential, freedom, and criminal prosecution (*SBA Research, 2021*).

According to reports, BITCRIME helped in several Dark Web drug cases in both Austria and Germany. In these cases, drug criminals made various transactions related to their illegal activities. By using advanced detection algorithms, BITCRIME's operators managed to construct a chain of transactions related to these cybercriminals and eventually identify names and places. This has resulted in the prosecution of dozens of criminals and the disruption of drug criminal gangs.

More fluid jurisdictional laws and shared data

Drug revenue continues to be the main source of income for a number of organized crime organizations. However, as with any illegal economic activity, drug dealers must find new ways to launder their cash, and they have gotten more inventive in the process. A modernized anti-drug strategy must put an emphasis on eradicating corruption through a comprehensive approach that involves bolstering governmental institutions, advancing human rights, decreasing impunity, reducing income inequality, and boosting educational systems. A group, representing civil society, academia, and policymaking and business communities in the whole world, must produce an initial series of suggestions on the following topics:

- Trade and integration in the economy
- Fighting drug trafficking and organized crime
- Increased international cooperation in fighting corruption
- Expanding and upgrading educational facilities across the board
- International drug trafficking operations and support for ongoing investigations
- Intelligence on drug trafficking routes that have been criminally analyzed
- Global police training should be upgraded to properly combat drug trafficking

Any analysis of Dark Web markets must obviously take practical and methodological considerations into account. Despite these drawbacks, the information in this chapter enables us to make certain inferences that back up actionable suggestions. Given the rapid rate of development in this field, it is vital to note that any recommendations will need to be reviewed on a regular basis. Next, conclusions and recommendations are grouped together based on their usefulness to monitoring and research, policy development, and practice in law enforcement:

- Established and robust pro-active policing approaches, taking place in a technologically collaborative and coordinated manner, are likely to be significant components if police activities are to have a sustained impact.

- There is a need for increased investment and capacity building. Various countries often come across huge skills gaps for performing investigations on the Dark Web, and many police authorities lack people who have expertise in operational drug-related criminal activities.

- Authorities must use a multi-agency strategy to focus on drug trafficking in order to stop activities from migrating to new or other existing marketplaces. This implies the need to prioritize other high-level threats and/or targets (big vendors or their suppliers), cooperate with the industry, and devise other measures in addition to targeting specific marketplaces.

- In order to use the expertise held beyond the purview of law enforcement to discover new threats and defeat existing ones, engagement with the private sector and the research community is also expected to become more crucial.

The criminal justice system has made some success in putting a stop to the sale of illegal goods and services on the Dark Web. Popular Dark Web markets such as Silk Road and Hansa have been deactivated since 2013. However, cybercrime happens quickly. There are still many Dark Web marketplaces, and some offenders have even started using Telegram and WhatsApp, two encrypted messaging services, to do their business. Due to the rapid evolution of Dark Web crime, law enforcement frequently finds itself playing catch-up.

The impact of the Dark Web on drug trafficking

Although individual drug markets typically don't last very long, the industry as a whole has overcome a number of obstacles such as law enforcement intrusions and exit scams. However, since the shutdown of Silk Road, transactions have tripled, and earnings have increased by half, despite the fact that the amount of the drug trade on Dark Web platforms is still quite tiny compared to offline trading. While decreasing many of the risks connected with offline markets (such as violence), the internet has provided chances for drug entrepreneurs to develop new business models and access a new user base while also introducing new risks (for example, postal interception and scams). The following screenshot presents the lifetimes of some specific marketplaces as well as the reasons behind their closures (*Goldsmith, 2020*):

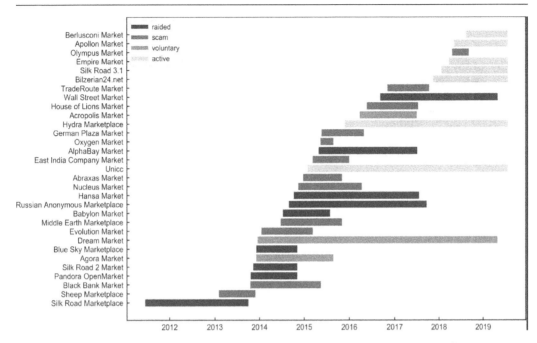

Figure 3.5 – Lifetimes of specific Dark Web drug markets (Rusnac et al., 2020)

Vendors can contact clients and accept payments anonymously thanks to encryption technologies. Vendors and customers never have to interact in person because the drugs are delivered via postal services. This shields the suppliers from a variety of dangers that are common in traditional drug distribution methods, such as undercover police, predatory stand-over tactics where suppliers risk being robbed, attacked, or even killed by rivals, and clients who might reveal their supplier if caught. On the Dark Web, additional hazards including client fraud and exit scams are seen as unavoidable but potentially controllable. According to some survey participants, the Dark Web's lack of physical risk may entice individuals who would not otherwise be willing to sell narcotics in addition to benefiting current drug providers.

Future studies should concentrate on identifying the characteristics of drug markets as well as offering advice on investigative tactics, situational drug prevention, and collaborations. There are a number of risks that could make it more difficult to respond to digitally facilitated drug transactions, including the emergence of new encryption technologies and decentralized software, new collection and delivery methods, deeper integration of Darknet markets with already established local drug markets, and an increase in the popularity of GPS-enabled apps.

It is still uncertain and ambiguous how much the influence of the worldwide market for illicit narcotics has been affected by internet-facilitated drug dealing. There is evidence to say that Dark Web drug markets are fueling offline markets for illegal drugs, but more work is required to fully comprehend the extent to which online buyers of drugs are distributing them offline. Finally, there are various discussions about the societal impacts of Dark Web dark markets. Some claim that dark markets lessen the amount of violence that occurs along the drug supply chain, which may be considered a beneficial outcome. Others, however, contend that crypto markets mostly have negative effects since they provide a new, frequently young customer base with simple access to the world of drugs. Nevertheless, every one of us can help to prevent drug trafficking in the following ways:

- Be aware of grooming tactics used by drug traffickers

- Educate ourselves on the characteristics of drug traffickers

- Parents can build strong and supportive relationships with their children

- Report a drug trafficking incident in the following agencies: **Federal Bureau of Investigation in the US (FBI)**, **Central Intelligence Agency in the US (CIA)**, **National Crime Agency in the UK (NCA)**, **European Union Agency for Law Enforcement Cooperation (Europol)**, and **International Criminal Police Organization (Interpol)**

Summary

Drug markets on the Dark Web offer consumer incentives and protection that are not available in regular street markets. The literature implies that the drug industry will continue expanding into virtual spaces since these incentives are mostly responsible for determining buyer motivation. Law enforcement faces considerable difficulties in identifying, controlling, and closing down these markets. Governmental agencies, civil society, academia, the commercial sector, regional police organizations, and international law enforcement must all keep researching and expanding their knowledge on Dark Web drug markets. The next chapter discusses the impact that Dark Web child pornography has on society.

4

Child Pornography on the Dark Web

The expansion of the World Wide Web and mobile technologies has helped people easily connect with pornographic material. Nowadays, the digital sexual market is rapidly growing, with material being shared, sold, and discussed on a global scale. On the other hand, material sexually exploiting children is on the rise in the digital world, despite significant efforts by governments and large corporations to restrain it. Additionally, the level of violence associated with crimes involving the sexual abuse of children has increased dramatically. Tragically, the only thing we've seen a decrease in is the victims' age. The online sexual abuse of children has long been a critical issue in our society. Child pornography is today seen, in many cultures, as a particularly heinous crime. According to certain figures, the COVID-19 pandemic has only made matters worse, with international law enforcement officials observing an increase in the usage of the Dark Web for sexual offenses against children (Europol, 2021). This chapter aims to address a variety of topics, including the following:

- Sexual abuse and sexual exploitation of children terms

- The issues surrounding child exploitation on the Dark Web

- Investigating the characteristics of anonymous users who engage in sexual activity with children

- Offenders' behaviors, tactics, and methods

- Efforts to reduce child abuse on the Dark Web

Analysis of these topics can reveal previously unknown information about the traits of suspects, their reasons for using the Dark Web, the type of criminal activity they are engaging in, their sexual preferences, and the nature of their interactions with one another. The results are explored in light of their theoretical and practical ramifications, as well as potential research avenues.

Child sexual abuse and child sexual exploitation terms

The Dark Web is the perfect sanctuary for child abusers. Sites such as *Lolita City*, *Hard Candy*, *Jailbait*, *Love Zone*, *PedoEmpire*, *Kindergarten Porn*, and *The Family Album* allow pedophiles to connect, share fetishes, practice child abuse techniques, and, most disturbing, exchange detailed methods on ways of finding, procuring, and seducing, and engaging in violent sexual acts with minors. The previous websites demonstrate thousands of producers of child exploitation material who rape and brutalize children for the satisfaction of pedophiles all over the globe (*Murali, 2019*). The volume of these sick activities is extraordinary and beyond any human imagination.

Despite the fact that **Child Sexual Abuse Material** (**CSAM**) is a worldwide problem, the United States continues to be one of the top producers of child abuse content with a very large user base. More than 150,000 children are trafficked per year for sex by pimps in the United States alone, and traffickers earn up to $200,000 per child each year. A horrific Europol report states that numerous Dark Web sites stream the live rape and abuse of children. Specifically, pedophiles in various European and Asian countries connect to live streams where they order abusers to perform sadistic actions on children. There is no documented evidence to prove the crimes occurred because the images are only live-streamed and not downloaded (*Gupta, 2021*).

According to reports from the **National Crime Agency** (**NCA**), the United Kingdom is in the grip of a corrosive and chronic threat from serious cybercrime. As of today, more than 150,000 people in Britain are viewing child sex abuse images by using the Dark Web. Lynne Owens, the former Director General of the National Crime Agency, stated: *"Improving our capacities is essential for the security of our country. If we don't, the public and the entire UK law enforcement community will suffer. Today's organized criminals are indiscriminate; they don't care what kind of crime they commit as long as it results in a profit. These organizations target those in society who are least able to defend themselves, such as young children and the elderly"* – (*Barnes, 2019*).

Dark Web child pornography is a relatively new phenomenon. However, the sexual abuse of minors is not. The sexual exploitation of children has existed for as long as humans have existed and there is a long history of the creation of drawings and sexual literature involving children (*Goldner, 2021*). Typically, pictures of kids with their genitalia exposed or in provocative positions are those that are deemed pornographic. Pictures and videos that have disturbing content involving children would also be considered child pornography. Usually, such pictures and videos show adults sexually abusing youngsters, including rape (Goldner, 2021). The law considers indecent photographs to be child pornography and forbids it if the following conditions are met:

- The photographs are obscene or sexually suggestive in nature
- The photographs particularly focus on a child's genitalia or anal area
- The photographs are extremely offensive and disturbing

Advanced technology has been used by those who abuse and/or sexually exploit children, as well as by those who have a sexual interest in kids. The convenience and expansion of the internet lie parallel to the growth of the child pornography market. Almost every internet-based technology, including social networking sites, gaming gadgets, file-sharing platforms, and even mobile apps, has easy access to child pornography photos (*Haasz, 2015*). In recent years, there has been discussion about changing the term *child pornography* to one that more correctly describes what is actually happening. The phrase *child pornography* may indicate that the child had some volitional involvement in the creation of sexual content. As a result, when discussing child pornography, law enforcement, organizations, researchers, and academics frequently use the terms *child sexual exploitation* or *child sexual abuse* (*Westlake, 2020*). These expressions assert the innocence of the victims in the material's production and rightly eliminate the idea of agency. The following table distinguishes the terms that are used when discussing child pornography (*Interpol, 2020*):

Type of abuse/exploitation	Definition
Child Sexual Abuse	Interactions or contact between a kid and an elder or more knowledgeable kids or adults (that is, outsiders, siblings, or persons in a position of authority such as parents or caretakers). In these situations, the other child or adult is using the innocent child (as an object) for their own sexual fulfillment. These interactions or contact involve the use of coercion, threats, deception, bribery, or other forms of pressure against the child.
Child Sexual Exploitation	Child sexual assault and/or other sex actions involving children are referred to as child sexual exploitation. It entails some sort of exchange (that is, drugs, affection, food, or shelter). There is frequently a connection between the phrases child sexual abuse and child sexual exploitation.
Online Child Sexual Abuse and Online Child Sexual Exploitation	Involve the sexual abuse and/or exploitation of children through the use of the internet.

Figure 4.1 – Distinction between child sexual abuse/exploitation terms

The child sex abuse industry causes children to suffer genuine, long-lasting harm. Due to the physical abuse and grooming that take place to make **child sexual exploitation** (**CSE**) content, as well as the knowledge that the material is constantly being shared online, children suffer from great emotional distress. Fighting this type of crime is also tricky for prosecuting authorities. Police authorities responsible for investigating sexual crimes against children may experience excessive stress and are at risk of various mental health disorders, including depression, burnout, and psychosis (*Brady, 2012*).

In regard to child abuse/exploitation, a thorough analysis identified 10 levels of severity. These levels are based on the rise in sexual victimization, and they purposefully include images that do not meet the criteria for child pornography as defined by the law. These 10 severity levels can be summarized as follows (*Aslan, 2011*):

- **Level 1**: Indicative (sexualized/non-erotic pictures)
- **Level 2**: Nudist (semi-naked or naked in legitimate sources/settings)
- **Level 3**: Erotica (stealthy photographs showing nakedness/underwear)
- **Level 4**: Posing (intentional posing with sexual content)
- **Level 5**: Sexy posing (deliberate sexual or provocative poses). The psychological significance that the child's image plays in arousal and masturbation is what gives it importance to the adult.
- **Level 6**: Explicit erotic posing (emphasis on the genitalia)
- **Level 7**: Explicit sexual activity (an explicit activity that does not involve an adult)
- **Level 8**: Assault (sexual assault that involves an adult)
- **Level 9**: Gross assault (penetrative assault that involves an adult)
- **Level 10**: Sadistic/bestiality (sexual images that involve pain or an animal)

It is crucial to stress that even Level 1 images can be sexualized and the subject of fantasies, and that they can be used to both encourage and sustain sexual imagination when discussing collections of photos. Even though the lines between the types of images can often be blurry, this typology takes into account the wide range of content that appeals to adults with a sexual interest in children and puts the focus back on the child as a victim rather than the finished obscene image. This is especially significant in the context of Level 3 images (pictures that are secretly taken). The severity of victimization is not diminished by the subject's ignorance of it.

The way that children and pornography are defined legally varies greatly between jurisdictions. The age at which people are legally allowed to engage in sex varies around the world depending on how the term *child* is defined. This makes it harder to manage child pornography cases internationally. Additionally, the concept of a child for child pornography purposes is distinct from the age of consent. For instance, depictions of anyone under the age of 18 are considered child pornography in the United States, although the age of consent can be as low as 14 in various jurisdictions.

Offenders' behaviors, tactics, and methods

Child pornography offenders like to lurk on Dark Web forums to share their interests, desires, fetishes, and experiences abusing children, in addition to sharing, trading, and selling images. Also, offenders enjoy watching other people who are blatantly exploiting children in the most brutal ways. Dark Web communities related to individuals with an attraction to **Child Sexual Exploitation Material** (**CSEM**) give users access to the following:

- Child sexual abuse content

- A chance to connect with like-minded people

- A feeling of acceptance and belonging

- A place where sexual fetishes can be communicated, confirmed, and satisfied

There have been various reports on the features of Dark Web child sex offenders, and there have been online forums, communities, and platforms for people with a sexual attraction to children for a long time now. For instance, one piece of research compared studies on offenders who utilize the internet to commit their offenses to offenders who come into sexual contact with children – and discovered that online offenders were in most cases younger in age and members of a minority ethnic group. Additionally, it was found that online offenders displayed more behaviors that are considered socially acceptable, reported fewer cognitive problems, such as fewer emotional similarities to children, and were less likely to have a history of physical abuse. They were less likely to be, or have been, married and more likely to report having been victims of sexual abuse when compared to the general population.

Furthermore, Dark Web forums devoted to CSEM have sizable membership groups. Seven forums contained over 2 million different user IDs. There were more than 300,000 users among the seven sites, notwithstanding the fact that some users register on multiple boards. Enhancing police authorities' comprehension of the risks posed by these forums' users has been designated as a significant goal in light of these findings, as has the prioritization of users suspected of participating in CSEM in order to identify them and stop their offending behavior (*Europol, 2016*).

While CSEM offenders who use communication sites on the Surface Web for their criminal activity have long been the subject of research, there is much less information available about, and comprehension of, their criminal activity when using such sites on the Dark Web. These Dark Web systems are not areas of the internet that are discovered by accident due to their very nature. A potential member must undergo vetting before being allowed access to certain forums and other restricted areas, which requires them to submit fresh CSEM material both when applying for membership and whenever it is renewed. Given the effort required to enter such forums and/or other restricted locations, one may therefore anticipate that those who use them are highly driven to offend. The Dark Web is the central platform for communication sites with specialized sexual fetishes, such as CSEM that involves extremely young children and sadism (*Europol, 2014*), and restricted sections are linked to talks and content that are much more aggressive and sadistic in nature (*Europol, 2020*). People who use the Dark Web for CSEM-related activities may display more aberrant sexual preferences than those who use the Surface Web since they are less likely to find an appropriate outlet there.

Child sexual exploitation on the Dark Web is not always an organized phenomenon in the traditional sense. In some cases, offenders act on their own, and there is little or no involvement by conventionally organized gangs. However, offenders do organize themselves (*Cipolla, 2014*). They congregate on Dark Web forums where they not only share and distribute CSEM but also discuss techniques and methods on how to avoid law enforcement detection. Such communities normalize offenders' behaviors and provide validation and encouragement, thus decreasing the likelihood of people with a sexual interest in children seeking help (*Europol, 2018*). The following figure shows a crime script of how child offenders operate on the Dark Web (*Leclerc et al., 2021*):

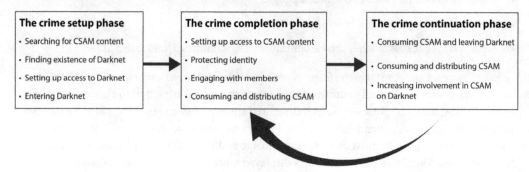

Figure 4.2 – Crime script of CSAM offenders operating on the Dark Web

Analysis of these actions reveals previously unknown information about the traits of suspects, their reasons for utilizing the Dark Web, the type of criminal activity they are engaging in, their ways of avoiding detection, their sexual preferences, and the nature of their contact with other offenders.

Efforts to reduce child abuse on the Dark Web

In order to combat abuse on the Dark Web, jurisdictional laws and shared data need to be more fluid. This can be done by sharing evidence with other relevant organizations, with the end goal of bringing child abusers and traffickers to justice. Although there are various methods of combating child exploitation on the Dark Web, they all have flaws to some extent, including advanced law enforcement tools.

Generally speaking, the police have a difficult time trying to identify those who create, distribute, and sell child exploitation material on the Dark Web. Criminal activity of this nature frequently involves many jurisdictions, making detection and punishment very challenging. Dark Web child sexual exploitation is still the most disturbing aspect of cybercrime and the amount of CSE material found on the Dark Web continues to grow. Child sexual abuse existed much earlier than the creation of the internet. However, the online dimension of this crime has enabled pedophiles to interact with each other and cause even more harm. This creates severe challenges for police investigations and victim identification efforts.

Project Arachnid

In 2016, in a quest to reduce CSE material on the Dark Web, the Canadian Centre for Child Protection introduced an automated website crawler called *Project Arachnid*. This tool has the ability to crawl the internet for known images of child sexual abuse material and trigger removal notices to big technology companies (*Project Arachnid, 2021*). The following figure shows some significant statistics about this tool:

As of October 1, 2021:

130 billion+ images processed

41 million+ images triggered for analyst review

9 million+ notices sent to providers

85% of the notices issued relate to victims who are not known to have been identified by police

Figure 4.3 – Canadian Project Arachnid statistics

Project Safe Childhood

Another great initiative in regard to the efforts made to fight the growing problem of child exploitation is *Project Safe Childhood*, launched in May 2006 by the US Department of Justice. This project's main goal is to better apprehend, locate, detect, and arrest people who exploit children by using the internet. Additionally, this project aims to investigate and prosecute vigorously, as well as to protect and assist victimized children. At the same time, this initiative recognizes the need for a broad, community-based effort to protect children around the world and guarantee future generations a safe place to live (*United States Department of Justice, 2022*).

Stop Child Abuse – Trace an Object

Additionally, the *Stop Child Abuse – Trace an Object* campaign was introduced by Europol on May 31, 2017. With this campaign, the audience was asked to identify objects seen in the backdrop of CSEM footage (*Europol, 2018*). People can anonymously submit information about objects without coming into contact with Europol or other law enforcement organizations. The recognition of these objects can potentially narrow down the location of the abuse, and it may be crucial in identifying the offenders or victims. Sharing images of these objects with the public helps to open them to a broader audience and allows anyone with information to leave comments. Such an approach has yielded significant results in the past (*Europol, 2021*).

Since the launch of Europol's campaign, more than 570 reports have been sent to the police. After more than 5 years, the reports received so far have been proven to be of tremendous value, resulting in the following (*ACCCE, 2021*):

- Three investigation leads
- Reports of abuse from members of the public who saw released images online
- Vendors of specific objects assisting with investigations
- Other reports of child sexual abuse (unrelated to the images) have been submitted on the campaign's main website

Regardless of the results of this campaign, the most important thing about this effort is that the images have resulted in increased awareness and discussion about Dark Web child sexual exploitation among the community (*ACCCE, 2021*). This campaign may not be the ultimate solution to combating online child exploitation, but it is a positive step forward.

MFScope

MFScope's primary objective is to offer a comprehensive analysis of cryptocurrency use on the Dark Web with a focus on illicit transactions. However, due to three key obstacles, reaching this goal is by no means a simple undertaking. First, because the Dark Web is anonymous, it can be challenging to gather cryptocurrency-related data from there. Second, because cryptocurrency addresses are *pseudonymous*, it is challenging to determine who owns them. Third, even if data on crypto transactions can be effectively gathered, more data is required to reveal users' identities for additional research. The following figure shows MFScope's workflow:

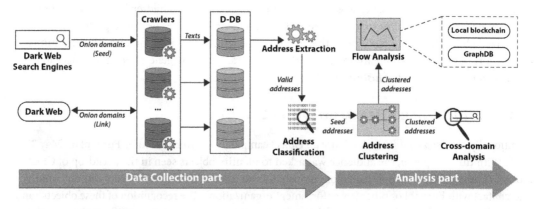

Figure 4.4 – MFScope's workflow

By using Ahmia, a TOR network indexing tool, and crawling collected hidden services, MFScope's technology extracts seed onion domain addresses. To increase the corpus of captured data, the program also extracts links to other hidden services from the crawled data. The infrastructure used by MFScope has allowed its creators to capture around 27 million dark website pages as well as 10 million distinct bitcoin addresses. The creators think that because of the extensive data collection method, their analysis is quite reliable. Due to the difficulty in determining the precise size of the Dark Web, they do not assert that their data covers the majority of cryptocurrency use cases on the Dark Web. Nevertheless, they argue that by analyzing a vast amount of data, it is possible to develop a reasonable understanding of how cryptocurrencies are used on the Dark Web.

Collaborative approach

When thinking of a collaborative approach, the primary objective is to combine reliable information sources and advanced tools in order to respond to abuse with agility and speed. When looking at the available tools, some of which were mentioned in previous chapters, many of them are distinguished into five categories: *Database Management*, *Image Recognition*, *Reporting*, *Awareness*, and *Deep Learning and Artificial Intelligence* (*AI*). In May 2019, the **US Center for Mind and Culture** (**CMAC**) released a paper regarding the top 40 technology tools that are used to combat child abuse and exploitation. Out of the 40 tools, 20 of them are available for public use, while the remaining are utilized by law enforcement, non-profit organizations, and private businesses (*Kennedy, 2019*).

The image recognition tools support a wide range of use cases, including facial recognition, video fingerprinting, advert scanning, and illegal content recognition. When comparing the list of available tools, it is apparent that some of them operate in regions such as the US, Canada, and China. Combining all the tools centrally will make the search by region more efficient, as it will enable more advanced international search options related to Dark Web child abuse. Powerful tools such as the Fess Crawler, an Elasticsearch-based server, can be configured to search for the most relevant information, for example, abusers' names and victims' identities (*Whittaker, 2017*).

The awareness section of a collaborative approach is aimed mainly at the general public. It can include websites, apps, games, and **Virtual Reality** (**VR**) to make resources on the signs of child abuse more easily accessible. The proposed collaborative approach can utilize built-in analytics and a central content management system. With that said, the analytics could help trace how awareness tools are shared through a central database/system – in the form of adverts, social media, promotions, and so on. They could also be used to check the number of users who "responded" to adverts by clicking on them or finishing the respective game or video. Additionally, there could be an option to show awareness statistics by region and compare that to crime reports to evaluate the efficiency of the system over time. A central content management system can be used to update the system's awareness section.

After awareness, the reporting process comes into place. Reporting tools can be focused on providing witness reports related to Dark Web child abuse crimes. The central system can have analytics that are capable of processing reports with assigned severity metrics, the number of similar reports in an area, as well as witnesses' trustworthiness based on previous reports. There are good examples of apps that are used for reporting child abuse-related incidents – the STOP App (UK), NAPTIP (Nigeria), and CyberTipLine (US). Having reports available centrally enables more powerful and robust international searching and tracing (*Smith, 2018*).

Database management tooling is associated with global data hubs and serves as networks that collect information on child abuse. In the context of the central database/system, collaboration and searching through regional databases are proposed as central solutions. Having the ability to engage the community on a specific Dark Web child abuse case, for example, asking a question in a hub's forum to see if people noticed a particular event or sending a push notification to subscribed users in the region, might be a useful step towards fighting this kind of crime.

In conclusion, deep learning and AI can provide an impressive set of tools to combat Dark Web child abuse. Also, a number of organizations, such as *Seattle Against Slavery*, work to target, deter, delay, and gather data about potential buyers of child abuse victims. Additionally, existing advanced algorithms can trace child abusers by identifying non-consensual sex ads, linking similar writing styles across ads, and uncovering cryptocurrency transactions (*The Lantern Project*, 2021).

Keep in mind that child abuse frequently occurs again in the following generation (*NCTSN, 2022*). Doing what you can to stop it now can help save children's lives and the generations that follow. Any family, any neighborhood, and any community can experience child abuse. According to studies, child abuse has no borders in terms of wealth, color, ethnicity, or religious conviction (*NSPCC, 2022*). The following are ways that ordinary people can help in order to prevent child abuse and exploitation:

- **Volunteer your time**: Cooperate with other parents in your area. Aid families and young children who are in need. Set up a playgroup.

- **Discipline your children thoughtfully**: Never discipline your child when you are enraged. Allow yourself some downtime to unwind. Do not overlook the role that punishment plays in educating your child. By using time-outs, and privileges to promote good behavior, you can aid your child in regaining control.

- **Educate yourself and others**: Offering straightforward support to children and parents may be the simplest way to stop child abuse. There are several strategies to shield kids from violence, such as after-school play, parent education classes, mentoring workshops, and respite care. Promote these programs in your neighborhood by acting as an advocate.

- **Know the signs**: There are other indications of maltreatment besides unexplained wounds. Depression, anxiety about a particular adult, lack of social skills or trust in others, abrupt changes in eating or sleeping habits, poor hygiene, inappropriate sexual behavior, secrecy, and hostility are frequent indicators of family issues and may be signs of the neglect or physical, sexual, or emotional abuse of a child.

Child sex abuse is likely happening in the city you live in. It may even be happening in your neighborhood, one street away. It may even be happening to someone you know. For this reason, it is of vital importance to know and understand the signs of child abuse in order to limit this terrible crime.

Summary

Investigation and punishment are difficult because of the international scope of child sex abuse on the Dark Web. Law enforcement authorities, governmental institutions, and non-profit groups are compelled to develop tools, adjust legislation, and establish the most effective techniques for combating this type of severe crime as technologies for making and spreading CSE content improve and expand. Although it is nearly impossible to completely eradicate CSE content, distribution can be managed through collaboration and the application of cutting-edge technologies. Collaboration between the commercial sector, the academic community, and civil society is necessary to combat online child sex abuse. Particularly, collaboration with the private sector, for example, **Internet Service Providers (ISPs)**, can help to limit access to CSEM and divert potential offenders from consuming CSE content to seeking help with their disturbing preferences. The following chapter covers the issues surrounding human trafficking on the Dark Web.

5
Human Trafficking on the Dark Web

Human trafficking, also known as modern slavery, is a grim reality of the 21st-century global landscape. This type of crime is considered the third most prevalent type of crime worldwide (*Homeland Security Today*, *2020*). On any given day, around 40.3 million people are victims of human trafficking, 4.8 million of them because of *forced sexual exploitation*. Human trafficking deprives millions of their dignity and freedom and leaves them vulnerable to abuse and violence. It even threatens international security and peace. Additionally, human trafficking benefits criminal organizations and terrorist networks and undermines law and world order. While traditional channels of human trafficking still exist, the Dark Web allows criminals to traffic a greater number of victims across larger geographical boundaries. In this chapter, we will cover the following topics:

- Types of human trafficking
- Offenders' behaviors, tactics, and methods
- Efforts to mitigate Dark Web human trafficking

Types of human trafficking

The advent of the internet and the part of it known as the Dark Web gave the opportunity to human traffickers to expand their business and make much bigger profits. So, this problem has taken on huge dimensions and, as a result, the various entities that are dealing with fighting human trafficking are not able to control the whole situation effectively. The appearance of the internet and the Dark Web is not the only reason why human trafficking has become a worldwide problem. Some of the main reasons human trafficking has expanded are as follows:

- Trafficking generates huge profits for traffickers
- The opportunity for repeated sale and sexual exploitation of children

- Systemic poverty and socioeconomic inequality

- Demand for cheap labor

- Lack of legitimate economic opportunities

- Conflict and war zones

There are several things that happen every day in this world. While a lot of things occur in public settings, a lot of things also take place behind closed doors—for example, sex trafficking, child pornography, gambling, and drug addictions, among many other events. Trafficking and sex trafficking, as well as the ways in which people are placed in such situations and the ways in which they are exploited, are among the many topics that our society does not particularly discuss nowadays. One example of how some people are exploited is through the sharing of child sexual abuse material and grooming. Many people are aware of what human trafficking and sex trafficking are, but we do not know if they also know that these crimes can also be connected to the Dark Web and that they can sometimes be hidden from view among the content that we come across every day on the internet.

The biggest problem with human trafficking and sex trafficking is that there is not enough information available about how they occur both offline and online. One or more of the main causes is that, while it may be publicly known, very few regular people actually observe and recognize human trafficking. Other important factors are the Dark Web's increasing involvement in ensuring that anyone can be trafficked, payment verification processes utilizing cryptocurrencies, and the Dark Web's evasiveness through its sophisticated algorithm for masking users' IP addresses. Nowadays, victims of trafficking are found online and are then transported by traffickers for their own selfish gain and exploitation. Additionally, there are still the traditional parts of trafficking that take place offline and feed its global expansion. With an estimated 40 million victims, there are several ways for traffickers to take advantage of other people.

Human trafficking involves the use of violence, manipulation, and false promises of well-paying jobs to lure victims into trafficking situations—for example, labor, slavery, and unwanted sexual acts. Blackmailing, threats, fear of their traffickers, and language barriers usually deter victims from seeking help (*Murali, 2019*). The following screenshot shows the primary forms of human trafficking (*StopTheTraffic, 2022*):

Figure 5.1 – Primary forms of human trafficking

Here is a list of statistics related to online human trafficking (*Equality Now, 2021*):

- The **National Center for Missing and Exploited Children** (**NCMEC**) estimates that 78 percent of online child sexual exploitation victims are girls

- In the US, two out of every three children sold for sex are trafficked on the internet

- In the UK, more than 8,500 sexual ads are posted online every month

- The Philippines Department of Justice receives more than 3,000 reports each month of children being sexually abused and sold online

The Dark Web is the ideal platform for human traffickers, as it is easy and cheap for them to buy, move, and exploit vulnerable men, women, girls, and boys (*Rhodes, 2000*). Host to hidden, password-protected sites, this dark side of the internet offers high anonymity to both traffickers and customers. Additionally, compared to traditional forms of trafficking, Dark Web trafficking has a lower chance of being discovered and prosecuted, which makes it an alluring and lucrative illicit business. Unlike other illegal activities—for example, the drug trade—with human trafficking, one victim can generate thousands of US dollars per day for criminals, as they can subject them to daily abuse and repeated sale (*Murali, 2019*). The following screenshot shows the most dominant forms of human trafficking among detected trafficked victims (*United Nations Office on Drugs and Crime, 2020*):

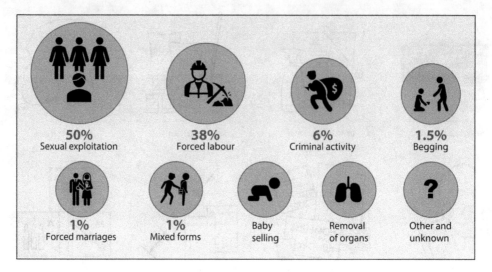

Figure 5.2 – Most dominant human trafficking forms among detected victims

The illegal business of Dark Web trafficking involves three main components:

1. Grooming and recruitment of vulnerable victims
2. The advertisement of illegal services
3. Payment for business expenses and services

Since a trafficking victim by definition does not consent to what is happening to them, the only way traffickers can succeed is by having full control over their victims. In some situations, it could seem as though the victim has given their consent, but a deeper look reveals that pressure, fraud, deception, or other unethical tactics were used to make the victim's consent ineffective. Numerous strategies are used by traffickers to maintain control over their victims. This mixture changes depending on the specific victim, the type of trafficking, the stage of the process, the location, and the opportunities provided by the environment. It is crucial to keep in mind that just because a victim has not experienced physical abuse does not mean they are not being kept under control.

Offenders' behaviors, tactics, and methods

On a massive scale, human trafficking happens all over the world. People who lack the resources and legal protection to protect themselves are subjected to forced labor or sexual coercion. The internet's reach is frequently used by cybercriminals who operate human trafficking rings to find potential customers for their services. To further their privacy, they use classified websites and Dark Web portals.

Offenders' behaviors

When seeking out or procuring victims, deception may be used (*It's bar work. There, the pay is excellent, and the work is simple.*). This could be combined with deception (*Don't let anyone know where you are going because we have to bribe someone to get a work permit. When you get paid, you can repay us.*). Some control mechanisms will become ineffective as the trafficking grows, or traffickers may need to alter their strategy and focus. It could be impossible to trick a victim after victims reach their destination (*There is no bar work. You have to labor in the fields.*). Control could deteriorate or get violent (*You are not appreciative. We don't like ungrateful people.* Or, *Work hard or my friend will beat you.*). Debt bondage is subject to change (*We bought your work permit. We now provide you with a place to sleep and eat. You owe us additional funds.*).

Traffickers may also offer *concessions* to keep their victims under control or lessen the likelihood that they would try to flee. Examples include brief periods of freedom, the ability for victims to retain a modest sum of money, or *privileges* such as making phone calls. Wherever concessions are made, there is frequently a strong threat lurking in the shadows—either direct or implicit.

The anonymity mechanisms offered by the Dark Web have created a space for pimps, traffickers, and customers to conduct their business with comfort and ease. Policing this space is extremely hard, and speculation around the use of the Dark Web as an enabler of human trafficking has inevitably been made in the past few years. Some people, particularly women, become involved in human trafficking as a result of their drug use, and they are connected to pimps who pay them for having sex with clients so that they can buy the narcotics they desire. On the Surface Web (the common internet to which everyone has access), there are several websites that promote human trafficking. Additionally, there are various kinds of pimps who convince girls to have relationships with them; many of the girls get involved because of survival sex, while others have escaped their homes or have drug addictions. The pimps offer the girls protection as well as a safe place to stay.

Human trafficking is not always characterized by victims leaving their country—it can include trafficking victims across local and state borders. One method used by pimps to exploit and control their victims after they have them in their grasp is to groom or develop a trusting rapport with the victim. These grooming methods are applied on all available online platforms, including chat rooms such as *WhatsApp*, dating services such as *Tinder*, *Bumble*, and *Hinge*, as well as instant messaging on *Twitter*, *Facebook*, and *Instagram*. The Polaris project's report on the demographics of reported trafficking victims for the year 2019 reveals that women make up the majority of victims; there is no conclusive information on the age at which trafficking starts, and the majority of those who are trafficked are unknown in terms of their citizenship status or their country of origin.

Offenders' tactics

Mobile devices and social media platforms, in particular, dramatically facilitate human trafficking. Mobile devices with web connectivity, for instance, enable these actions while maintaining some level of anonymity for the perpetrators. Many human trafficking cases involve the grooming and recruitment of defenseless victims through social networking sites such as *Instagram*, traffickers' websites, or other channels. It has been observed that human trafficking victims promote their services to potential clients on social networking and online classified advertising sites including *Craigslist, Backpage*, and *Facebook (Latonero, 2011)*. Both consumers and human traffickers use the ease of the Dark Web and credit cards to pay for business-related costs or services, such as reserving hotels or multiple rooms in different cities, posting online ads on adult websites, transferring money, buying fast food, using ride-sharing services, or purchasing airline tickets.

Digital and internet technology have impacted all forms of sex trafficking, which has also resulted in the birth of numerous new sorts *(Reid, 2016)*. The growth of child pornographic content, which has been demonstrated to expand both in terms of the number of creators and consumers as well as the quality of the material, has been attributed to the Dark Web's unprecedented technological accessibility and elevated level of anonymity. The sharing of images, recordings, and even live performances involving child sexual abuse and exploitation can be done today using a variety of internet technologies, such as websites, email, instant messaging, file-sharing networks, and social networking sites.

Producers of teen modeling photos and movies keep up with changes in state laws that govern what is permitted and prohibited, and they take advantage of any ambiguities to avoid being detained and prosecuted. Furthermore, in order to lure young teens into sex trafficking, human traffickers routinely pose as model agency scouts looking for *webcam models* on social media *(Latonero, 2011)*. While digital technology has changed the way that children are exploited for sexual purposes, other types of sex trafficking have also benefited from these developments. Most internet sex trafficking involves coerced prostitution or the prostitution of minors. Smartphones and computers are used by sex traffickers to facilitate crime in a variety of ways, including for victim recruitment, victim promotion, and communication with other criminals. The use of the internet to promote the sexual exploitation of others has increased recently; it is believed that 75 percent of minor sex trafficking in the US now takes place online, up from 38 percent in 2004.

Offenders' methods

Viewers of child exploitation material are able to connect to live-stream videos of children being sexually abused. During these live-stream videos, the viewers can make real-time requests. While the abuse takes place, consumers can buy instant gratification based on their sexual fetishes. This trend is also known as **Molestation On-Demand** (**MOD**). Furthermore, one example of globalism's impact is the emerging trend of webcam child sex tourism. It involves wealthy consumers, usually from the US or Western Europe, who virtually exploit children living in other countries *(Reid* and *Fox, 2020)*. According to statistics, 83 percent of pedophiles have sexual abuse photos of children under the age of 12, 39 percent of them have images of children under the age of 6, and 19 percent of them have images of children under the age of 3. Surprisingly, child sex traffickers might be acquaintances, family members, friends, or guardians, as well as total strangers. Family participation in cases of child trafficking is up to four times greater than in cases of adult trafficking, with over half of all recognized cases beginning with some form of family engagement. Sick pedophiles exchange tips on how to avoid police discovery and talk about online anonymity methods on the Dark Web.

There are over 2 million daily users on the Dark Web. It serves as the ideal haven for criminal organizations to communicate, advertise, and transact with anything, including human beings. The most alluring and profitable crime among them is human trafficking. According to studies conducted in the US over a 2-year period, traffickers spent roughly 250 million US dollars to publish over 60 million advertisements on somewhere between 30,000 and 40,000 Dark Web pages. Even drug trafficking cannot compete with it. According to a recent **United Nations** (**UN**) estimate, human trafficking generates $150 billion annually. Approximately 40 million individuals are being trafficked as this is being read, with more than half being women and girls and more than a million being minors, and up to 25 percent of them are purchased and sold as sex slaves (*Murali, 2019*).

One of the most notorious human trafficking gangs, known as the **Black Death Group** (**BDG**), also operates on the Dark Web. Allegedly, this group offers a variety of services, including the sale of sex slaves, the distribution of drugs and weapons, and bomb manufacturing (*Lawless* and *Barry, 2017*). One of their disclaimers says that they do not sell girls who are terminally ill, pregnant, have **sexually transmitted diseases** (**STDs**), or are young mothers. One case that got considerable attention was the kidnapping of the British model Chloe Ayling. According to reports, a BDG member lured Ms. Ayling to a fake studio in Milan, injected her with ketamine, and took her to an isolated place where she was tied up for 6 days. A few days later, the criminal was captured and faced trial in Italy (*Griffin, 2017*).

Efforts to mitigate Dark Web human trafficking

Human trafficking is a kind of crime that affects societies in all countries of the world. **ECPAT**, also known as **Every Child Protected Against Trafficking**, is the leading anti-trafficking organization in the US, and it belongs to a network of organizations that expands and operates in more than 100 countries. All these organizations work together to combat the commercial sexual exploitation of children. ECPAT-USA seeks to protect every single child's human right to grow with freedom and away from the threat of sexual exploitation and trafficking. ECPAT achieves this mainly through advocacy, awareness, education, and legislation. By using targeted advertisements, ECPAT promotes corporate responsibility in the private sector with a strong focus on tourism. Additionally, ECPAT empowers young individuals to take the lead against modern slavery by equipping them with the tools and knowledge necessary to help them become activists against human trafficking (**ECPAT-USA, 2022**).

In the last decade, modern slavery has gone dark and digital. Technology and globalization facilitate the dissemination of human trafficking by multiplying the opportunities and connections traffickers have to recruit and exploit humans. As with other criminals, human trafficking gangs do not play by the rules. Traffickers, who are frequently associated with international, transnational organized crime, use all the strategies described in the Dark Web book to escape detection and punishment, including cutting-edge encryption. Additionally, they are able to blend into the background by frequently changing between profiles and websites. However, authorities are fighting back and are now able to monitor all layers of the internet, including the Dark Web and covert TOR services, by utilizing advanced **artificial intelligence** (**AI**) algorithms and big data software (*Reid* and *Fox, 2020*).

Big tech companies' monitoring software enables law enforcement to spot human trafficking on the Dark Web and even communicate with traffickers completely anonymously, generating evidence that might be used against them in court. The intelligence platforms of these tech companies can be utilized to give real-time content monitoring with the ability to scan photos and texts—which provides unequaled situational awareness—with the seamless integration of advanced data sources. While some posts may appear to be hidden to the untrained eye, media intelligence platforms and online research tools can offer useful information in locating suspects and real-world risks of human trafficking (*Cobwebs, 2022*).

Intelligence-led policing

In the never-ending search for ways to combat human trafficking more effectively, one solution looks ideal—to prevent crimes from occurring in the first place. Since the 1990s, several law enforcement agencies worldwide have been using some form of intelligence-led approach to preventing crimes. In simple words, intelligence-led policing tries to promptly identify potential victims and repeat offenders (*LeCates, 2018*). Subsequently, by working in collaboration with the community, this approach attempts to provide offenders with an opportunity to alter their behavior before being arrested for a more severe crime.

One of the biggest obstacles to disrupting human trafficking on the Dark Web is the lack of intelligence into the inner workings, networks, and back stories—things that build a real-time picture of what is happening. The world needs an accurate global perspective, which can only occur with the coordinated gathering and sharing of data. Through the intelligence-led approach of sharing information about trends and hotspots, law enforcement agencies can disrupt the money flow, gather essential evidence for human trafficking investigations, and provide safer environments for vulnerable groups (*Sintelix, 2021*).

With the use of data and information, police agents of Europol and Interpol have managed to more effectively assess crime patterns and problems, enabling senior decision-makers to efficiently allocate resources and create crime-fighting plans related to human trafficking on the Dark Web. This information is converted into strategically useful knowledge in cooperation with several international police department units. In other words, this intelligence enables the implementation of appropriate actions, strategies, and resources in a certain manner. This leads to a targeted strategy to deal with certain criminal problems and offenders that trickles down to the investigators and police agents on the ground in the affected crime areas.

Pipl Search

Human trafficking rings have always been challenging to investigate. Usually, uncovering a few abusers is not enough to stop a whole ring's activity. Also, traditional human exploitation investigation methods are quickly becoming obsolete, and abusers find opportunities to exploit vulnerable humans on the Dark Web (*Zeid, Moubarak*, and *Bassil, 2020*). In order to successfully uncover both the identities and associations of abusers, investigators must search suspected abusers' addresses, email histories, social media accounts, and connections. One way to do this is by using the automated tool Pipl Search, a tool that makes deep correlations among billions of **unique identifiers** (**UIDs**) (*Pipl, 2021*).

Pipl's unparalleled global index of identity information allows law enforcement to make Dark Web crime connections that other companies cannot. The advanced software of Pipl can help law enforcement authorities significantly reduce the time spent on review and research. Forensic investigators can use Pipl Search to uncover the identities and associations of human traffickers, and also their behavioral patterns. Pipl's rich identity profiles can be probed for online public-facing, offline content, as well as for an abuser's known associates. The following screenshot shows the components of Pipl Search (*Pipl, 2020*):

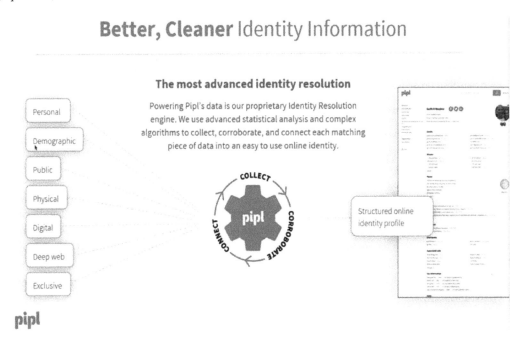

Figure 5.3 – Pipl's structure

In several instances, Pipl Search has helped police investigations in the fight of combating human trafficking on the Dark Web. This tool has been extensively used by international law enforcement, such as the FBI, and yielded significant results. The fast-paced results of Pipl Search help to narrow down results and conduct investigations in a more sophisticated manner. Pipl Search is so good that it even looks for references to names in public documents such as birth databases, **Securities and Exchange Commission** (**SEC**) filings, and real estate records. Additionally, it finds email addresses and compiles *quick facts* on the subject.

Banks and fintech

Another way of disrupting human trafficking on the Dark Web is with the collaboration of law enforcement with banks and different fintech companies to identify human trafficking-related transactions. Banks have a significant role to play because money flows globally. If you can track the money, you can track the people. The majority of traffickers utilize legitimate financial institutions in a variety of ways. Traffickers may use prepaid credit cards, make bank accounts for victims, or even encourage victims to transfer money using money remittance services (*Polaris, 2021*).

Most banks have established measures to fight money laundering, drug trafficking, terrorist financing, human trafficking, and a wide variety of other financial crimes. Additionally, banks and credit card companies have designed sophisticated systems for identifying potential human traffickers through patterns of payment, spending, travel deposits, and other ways of moving money. The following are some additional red flags for banks when it comes to identifying human traffickers (*Piazza, 2017*):

- Spending on suspicious websites
- Transactions in suspicious locations
- Excessive travel expenses
- Cash deposits at ATMs in multiple cities
- Excessive spending on food, lodging, or personal items

Furthermore, many nations have instituted banking regulations and criminalized money laundering in order to make it easier to detect and seize the assets of human trafficking activity. Prevention and detection are key factors against online financial crime. NatWest Group has invested more than 1 billion pounds in anti-money laundering systems and controls. At NatWest Group, the UK banking institution, they run processes, technologies, and platforms that help them know their customers, suppliers, and third parties. They monitor payments and all sorts of transactions, in order to effectively protect the customers, society, and the group, and when needed, they stop payments and close accounts where activity is suspicious or cannot be appropriately explained.

Collaborative approach

What has been discussed so far suggests that mitigating/preventing human trafficking on the Dark Web is not an easy task. Human trafficking is a hidden, widespread, and abhorrent crime with very deep roots in our society. It cannot be disrupted without a combination of sophisticated tools and practices, and the collaboration of various law enforcement authorities. Raising awareness regarding the dangers of trafficking and the signs to look out for is paramount to the overall effort of combating this kind of crime. Stopping these horrible deeds requires more than just being aware of the warning indicators of human trafficking. We can all do our share to aid victims of trafficking by learning more about the problem, spreading awareness, speaking up, and taking action. You'll be prepared to make a genuine impact whether you decide to volunteer, learn how to recognize signs of trafficking in your neighborhood, or make stopping trafficking your life's work through a committed career.

Summary

The problem of human trafficking is still growing and changing. It is slowly but surely moving more and more online in terms of how it is conducted. Although a minor proportion of trafficking currently happens on the Dark Web, there are still other avenues that do not require a connection to the Dark Web in order to contact trafficking victims, according to accumulating data. The majority of people are aware of human trafficking and what the Dark Web is, but more education is required regarding the operation of TOR technology and the motivations behind some users' use of that web browser. Massive efforts have been made in recent years to combat human trafficking. The characteristics of the Dark Web give law enforcement a digital setting where personnel can carry out forensic investigations. In order to identify trends, patterns, and correlations connected to human trafficking on this nefarious side of the internet, police enforcement can analyze very massive datasets using cutting-edge methods. Cooperation between local, state, federal, and international law enforcement authorities is required since cases of Dark Web human trafficking frequently cross jurisdictional boundaries. The next chapter covers topics surrounding cyberterrorism on the Dark Web.

6

Cyberterrorism on the Dark Web

Terrorism, in its broadest sense, is an action or threat against persons or properties with the purpose of negatively influencing governments or intimidating the public. In most cases, the term *terrorism* involves the use of fear and violence in the pursuit of ideological, religious, and political aims. Some of the most well-known terrorist organizations are the *Islamic State of Iraq and Syria* (*ISIS*), the *Taliban*, and *Al-Qaida*. In the past few decades, terrorism has gone dark and digital. The term *cyberterrorism* was first mentioned by Dr. Barry Collin, and it describes a planned attack performed by terrorists on computer systems. Cyberterrorism can be found all over the internet, especially on the Dark Web. There has been a great deal of concern over the possible threat posed by cyberterrorism. The threat of cyberterrorists breaking into public and private computer networks and destroying the military, financial, and service sectors of countries has been widely highlighted by security professionals, academics, lawmakers, and others. This chapter will cover the following cyberterrorism topics:

- What is terrorism?
- Why do terrorists use the Dark Web?
- How do terrorists operate on the Dark Web?
- Countering Dark Web terrorism

What is terrorism?

On the worldwide networks that exist, new security threats and weaknesses are exposed as technology is increasingly ingrained in society. One of the greatest potential security dangers around the globe is cyberterrorism. It has surpassed the development of nuclear weapons and contemporary international crises in importance. Digital weapons represent a threat to entire economic or social institutions because of how prevalent the internet is and how much responsibility is put on it. There are various types of cyberterrorists. We can categorize them into four primary groups, as shown in *Figure 6.1*.

The first group is comprised of active terrorists who are actively planning attacks or making changes to certain websites. They launch a cyberattack using a computer network as a tool, then they utilize the attack as a weapon. Terrorist sympathizers fall into the second category; while lacking full information, they take part in terrorist activities because they hold the same views as the terrorist organization that is behind these crimes. The third category includes involved states or nations that participate in terrorist acts in order to develop specific cyberwarfare capabilities. The last type is joyriders, which include individuals who utilize terrorism and cyberattacks to get famous:

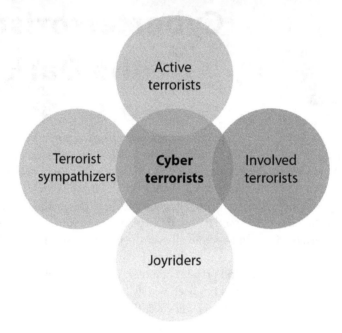

Figure 6.1 – Cyberterrorist categories

In nations with intermediate political freedom, terrorism is more common. On the other hand, in most democratic nations, terrorism is the least common. A terrorist's ability to take over, control, or alter the monitoring functions of governmental systems could threaten regional peace and sometimes international security. According to the **Global Terrorism Index (GTI)**, religious extremism has become the main driver of terrorist attacks worldwide. Terrorist attacks take place usually by using explosives. In this way, terrorists achieve maximum fear and publicity. The majority of the time, terrorist organizations meticulously plan their assaults in advance. They may also recruit victims, place undercover agents, and generate funds from sympathizers or through organized crime. The following screenshot shows the countries that had the highest number of deaths by terrorism in 2021 (*Statista, 2022*):

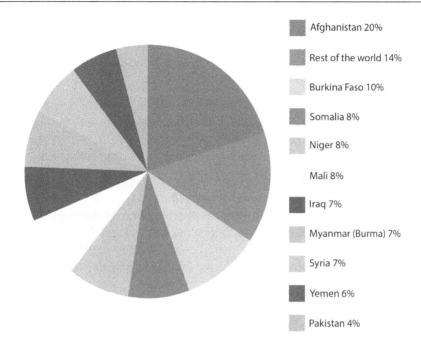

Afghanistan 20%

Rest of the world 14%

Burkina Faso 10%

Somalia 8%

Niger 8%

Mali 8%

Iraq 7%

Myanmar (Burma) 7%

Syria 7%

Yemen 6%

Pakistan 4%

Figure 6.2 – Countries with the highest number of deaths by terrorism in 2021

It is exceedingly unlikely that an extremist terrorist will harm anyone outside of a conflict zone. For instance, since 9/11, six Americans die each year at the hands of such terrorists in the US, which is significantly fewer than the number of individuals who drown in bathtubs. However, some contend that because anti-terrorism tactics are so successful, the frequency of terrorist destruction is limited. They further argue that, unlike bathtubs, terrorism offers no benefit and exacts costs far beyond those in the event itself by harmfully sowing fear and anxiety and by requiring policymakers to adopt countermeasures that are expensive and excessive.

Why do terrorists use the Dark Web?

The idea of cyberterrorism has its origins in the early 1990s when studies on the possible hazards posed by the highly networked, high-tech-dependent United States were first published in response to the debate surrounding the burgeoning *information society* and the rapid development in internet use. We are at risk, the National Academy of Sciences declared in a 1990 report on computer security. US and the world are becoming more and more reliant on computers, and a terrorist of the future could be able to cause more destruction with a keyboard than with a bomb. For modern terrorists, cyberterrorism conducted through the Dark Web is an attractive option for several reasons:

- **It is cheaper than traditional terrorist tactics**: Terrorists only need a computer and an internet connection. Instead of purchasing weapons such as guns and bombs, terrorists can construct and distribute computer viruses using phone lines, cables, Bluetooth technologies, or wireless connections.

- **It is more anonymous than traditional terrorist methods**: Terrorists, as with many internet users, go by *screen names* or access websites as anonymous *guest users*, making it very challenging for security organizations and law enforcement to identify the terrorists' true identities. Additionally, there are no actual obstacles in cyberspace, such as checkpoints, borders, or customs officers that must be avoided.

- **The variety and number of targets are enormous**: The computers and computer networks of organizations, people, public utilities, commercial airlines, and other entities could be among the many targets of a cyberterrorist. The sheer volume and complexity of prospective targets ensure that terrorists will be able to identify weak points and openings. According to numerous studies, key infrastructures such as electric power grids and emergency services are susceptible to cyberterrorist attacks because of how complicated the infrastructures and computer systems that run them are, making it practically hard to find and fix all flaws.

- **Cyberterrorism can be conducted remotely**: A quality that terrorists find especially alluring. Compared to traditional forms of terrorism, cyberterrorism needs less physical training, psychological commitment, risk of death, and traveling, making it simpler for terrorist groups to enlist and keep supporters.

- **Larger victim base**: Cyberterrorism has the ability to directly harm more people than more conventional terrorist tactics, which would lead to more media attention—which is ultimately what terrorists seek.

A combination of psychological, political, and economic elements has fueled a dread of cyberterrorism. Two of the main psychological concerns of modern society are combined in the term *cyberterrorism*. Fear of arbitrary, violent victimization goes hand in hand with skepticism and outright phobia of computer technology. A threat that is unknown is considered more dangerous than one that is. Cyberterrorism may not openly threaten violence, but it can nonetheless have a similar psychological effect on terrified societies. Furthermore, it is difficult to understand the genuine threat posed by cyberterrorism due to a lack of knowledge or, worse still, a surplus of fake information. The following diagram shows cyberterrorism's main elements:

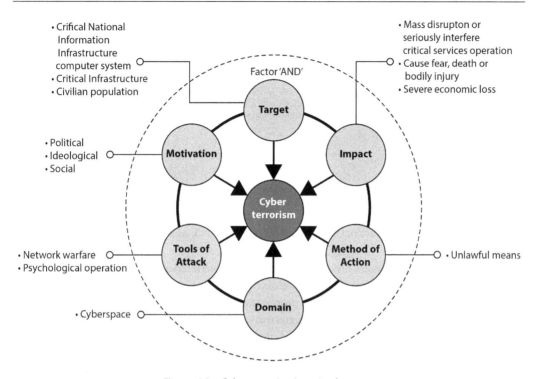

Figure 6.3 – Cyberterrorism's main elements

Nowadays, everyone has access to an immense amount of data in cyberspace. As many criminals do, terrorists have also taken advantage of the hidden part of the internet and its highly advanced technologies. Despite the long-held belief that terrorist strikes are organized through shadowy networks, the usage of Dark Web platforms by terrorists was only made clear in 2013. In particular, the **National Security Agency (NSA)** of the US intercepted digital conversations between Ayman Al-Zawahiri, the commander of Al-Qaeda, and Nasir Al-Wuhaysi, the leader of Al-Qaeda in the Arabian Peninsula, which has its base in Yemen, in August 2013. According to the Institute for National Security Studies, for roughly 10 years, at least some of the contact between Al-Qaeda network members took place on the Dark Web. The following screenshot shows the threats that Dark Web terrorism poses to national security and peace:

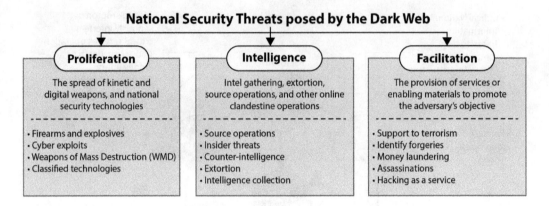

Figure 6.4 – National security threats posed by Dark Web terrorism

Despite the fact that the internet has brought many benefits to modern society, terrorists and terrorist organizations can also take advantage of this technology. Throughout the years, more citizens, especially young people, have much easier access to the propaganda of terrorist organizations and illicit acts, thanks to the internet and the Dark Web. Cyberterrorism is a contemporary form of terrorism that uses even more effective psychological warfare techniques to link terrorist operations with the virtual world. You never know who might become the next victim in the digital sphere. Various methods that terrorists are exploiting the Dark Web to further their cause have been discovered by numerous investigations. These encompass anything from psychological warfare and propaganda to incredibly useful purposes such as fundraising, recruiting, data mining, and action coordination. The following list highlights the use cases of the Dark Web for terrorist purposes:

1. **Terrorists use the Dark Web to hide**: Extremist content is being taken down from social media platforms at a higher pace as a result of social media corporations and security personnel monitoring the Surface Web. Growth in the use of the Dark Web by terrorist networks for communication, radicalization, dissemination of propaganda, and attack planning is correlated with this.

2. **Terrorists use the Dark Web for recruitment**: While first contact can be established on platforms that are part of the Surface Web, detailed instructions on how to access jihadist websites on the Dark Web are frequently provided on **end-to-end** (**E2E**) encryption apps such as *Telegram* and *WhatsApp*.

3. **Terrorists use the Dark Web as a way for propaganda**: The likelihood that terrorist groups' materials will be lost increases when extreme and terrorist information is removed from the Surface Web. A lot of this content later reappears on the Dark Web.

4. **Terrorists use virtual currencies to fundraise and evade detection**: Cryptocurrencies offer the same level of financial anonymity for terrorists and criminals that encryption does for communication systems.

The media, the information technology community, and the cybersecurity industry are all focused on the threat posed by cyberterrorism. Journalists, politicians, and professionals from a range of fields have identified signs in which highly skilled cyberterrorists use sophisticated tools to break into computers that manage air traffic control systems or dams, causing calamity and putting millions of lives in danger. By using the Dark Web, terrorists can plot their assaults, recruit new terrorists, and finance their activities. Hacking into public or private systems to gain access to confidential data or even to steal money for use in terrorism is the more common conception of cyberterrorism. The following list shows some examples of cyberterrorism on the Dark Web:

- Introduction of malware to corporate and public data networks

- Hacking of sensitive infrastructures to disrupt communication and steal sensitive data

- Causing inconvenience and financial losses by taking over websites and making them inaccessible to their intended users

- Attacks on banking institutions to steal money and cause terror

How do terrorists operate on the Dark Web?

Many people worry that cyberterrorism poses a serious threat to the economies of nations and that an assault may perhaps trigger another Great Depression. Since the late 1990s, terrorists can be found on several online sites. However, it was discovered that terrorists seeking the ultimate anonymity would find the Surface Web to be too perilous because they could be watched, tracked, and located. Many of the social media platforms and websites used by terrorists on the Surface Web are watched by anti-terrorism organizations, and they are frequently taken down or compromised.

On the Dark Web, however, decentralized and anonymous networks help terrorist sites avoid capture and closure. Beatrice Berton of the European Union Institute for Security Studies wrote in her report on ISIS's use of the Dark Web: "*ISIS's activities on the Surface Web are now being monitored closely, and the decision by a number of governments to take down or filter extremist content has forced the jihadists to look for new online safe havens.*" The unrestricted, anonymous, and easily available character of the Dark Web is exploited by terrorist organizations and those who support them to spread a variety of messages to a variety of targeted audiences through their dozens of websites and social networking sites.

More than ever before, terrorists are using the Dark Web to communicate. The Dark Web is widely utilized by terrorists, according to Bernard Cazeneuve, France's former prime minister, who made this claim in March 2016. He claimed during a National Assembly meeting that individuals responsible for the recent terrorist attacks in Europe used the Dark Web and encrypted platforms to communicate. ISIS started using the Dark Web to disseminate news and propaganda after the attacks in Paris in November 2015, ostensibly in an effort to conceal the names of the organization's supporters and defend its information from hacktivists. The claim was made following the removal of hundreds of websites linked to ISIS as part of the *Operation Paris* campaign.

Terrorists are continually looking for newer and more sophisticated applications and platforms in order to maintain their online presence on as many platforms as possible. Terrorists and their sympathizers still make use of the Hidden Wiki's free services, which is a list of a number of censorship-resistant TOR hidden services, despite the fact that browsing on the Dark Web is more challenging than it is on the Surface Web. On the Hidden Wiki's home page, there is a list of links to other websites. The Onion pseudo-top-level domain, which can only be accessed through TOR, is used by the service known as the *Hidden Wiki*. On its home page, there are links to a variety of clandestine services, such as links for money laundering, hired cyberattacks, contract killing, drugs, and bomb-making. The remainder of the wiki provides links to websites that include child pornography and abuse photographs.

Additionally, terrorists post material on the Dark Web explaining how they conduct their operations. For instance, the pro-Al Qaeda hacking group *Al-Qaeda Electronic* compromised five websites of major Austrian companies in July 2014. *Al-Maarek Media*, the organization's media arm, made a claim regarding the attack on its Dark Web account and social media profiles. Mirrors of the defacements and the URLs of the targeted websites were also included in the post. The same content that *Al-Qaeda Electronic* had previously used in attacks on a number of French, British, Norwegian, Russian, and Vietnamese websites was present on all of the compromised web pages. Later, in August 2015, a Dark Web forum known as *Turkish Dark Web* that included instructions in Turkish for constructing explosives and weapons and discussed the outcomes, potential applications, and usefulness of the tools.

Countering Dark Web terrorism

The ability to research and combat Dark Web terrorism has been hampered by the secrecy of this area of the web and the absence of practical methodology built for data collecting and analysis on the Dark Web. The possibility of cyberattacks from the Dark Web employing TOR networks was emphasized in IBM's security division's report on security threats for the third quarter of 2015. It is extremely essential to offer proof that the Dark Web has evolved into a significant hub for international terrorism and criminal activity in order to inspire the creation of the tools required to combat it. Based on the characteristics of cyberterrorism, it is possible to reconstruct the criminological dimensions of terrorist attacks on the Dark Web. But first, the following questions must be analyzed:

- Who are the offenders of cyberterrorism (whether the state discards them, whether they are supported by a state, whether they are quasi-public formations, people, or hacker groups in power who are engaged in espionage)?

- Which techniques and tools will be used when planning and executing an attack?

- How to apply the procedures, tactics, and techniques for performing cyberattacks (a method of social engineering, creation, and distribution of malware and viruses into a computer system)?

- Where is the attack carried out (banking and finance, information and communication networks, vital services of a country)?

- What is the motivation for carrying out the cyberattack, what do the terrorists want to achieve, and what are the advantages and disadvantages of such an action?

- When is the attack carried out?

One study used a variety of data and web mining technologies to provide the tools for thorough data collecting and analysis from the Dark Web. A long-term scientific research initiative, called the *University of Arizona-Dark Web* project, seeks to investigate and comprehend the phenomena of global terrorism using a computational, data-centric methodology. This project produced one of the largest libraries of extremist websites, forums, and multimedia files (images and videos), as well as social media postings worldwide over the years. However, new techniques and tactics for monitoring and assessing terrorist usage of the Dark Web are required given the increased sophistication of terrorists' use of the platform. The counterterrorism agencies' new and difficult mission is this.

Scientists from all around the world have been working on ways to combat terrorist activity on the Dark Web and in cyberspace for the past few years. Experts can locate, categorize, and examine online extremist activity using cutting-edge techniques including web crawling, link analysis, content analysis, authorship analysis, sentiment analysis, and multimedia analysis. One of the tools created by professionals on the Dark Web is the **Writeprint** technique (*Figure 6.5*), which automatically extracts thousands of linguistic and semantic data to ascertain who is authoring anonymous content online. The professionals also search conversation threads and other content using sophisticated tracking tools called web spiders to look for online forums where terrorist activity is occurring:

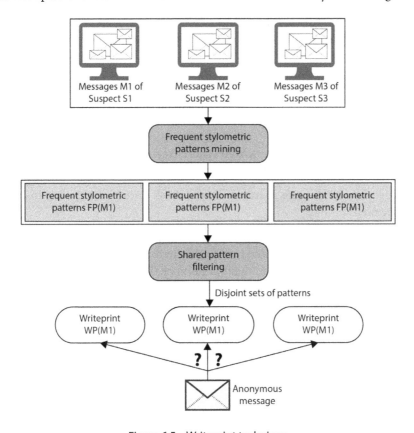

Figure 6.5 – Writeprint technique

The former US Homeland Security Secretary Michael Chertoff and the head of the Synergia Foundation in India Tobby Simon published a special report in February 2015 titled *The Impact of the Dark Web on Internet Governance and Cyber Security* that offered various recommendations addressing the Dark Web. In their study, Chertoff and Simon state that "*In order to formulate comprehensive strategies and policies for governing the Internet, it is important to consider insights on its farthest reaches — the deep Web and, more importantly, the dark Web*". They add that while the Dark Web may not have the same level of attractiveness as the Surface Web, this hidden part of the internet is conducive to planning, fundraising, and propaganda, which corresponds to the initial perception of the Dark Web as an unregulated marketplace. The report recommends the following efforts to monitor the Dark Web:

- Mapping the hidden services directory
- Hidden-service tracking of new sites for ongoing or later analysis
- Social site monitoring to find communication containing new Dark Web domains
- Semantic analysis to track future illicit activities and malicious actors
- Marketplace profiling to gather data about sellers, users, and the kinds of goods exchanged

The **United Nations Office on Drugs and Crime** (UNODC) concluded in its Annual Report that nations should take into consideration a universal agreement requiring countries to cooperate with each other during Dark Web cyberterrorism investigations. The UNODC stated that the absence of an international agreement on cybercrime and terrorism is impeding efforts to bring terrorists to justice. By putting into reality a number of suggestions, the report (*UNODC Annual Report, 2015*) urged national legislation to establish methods for combating cyberterrorists and for the successful prosecution of such instances:

- To gather *essential evidence* in Dark Web cyberterrorism investigations, law enforcement agencies should collaborate with ISPs.
- Wi-Fi network and cybercafé operators should think about forcing users to sign up and identify themselves.
- Because terrorists have access to the public internet, including airport and library Wi-Fi hotspots, national governments should criminalize terrorist conduct online by regulating ISP addresses in order to uphold human rights protections. **The Use of the Internet for Terrorist Purposes** is a new technical assistance tool that UNODC created and released in October 2012 in cooperation with the UN **Counter-Terrorism Implementation Task Force (CTITF)**. This technical help tool intends to give policymakers, investigators, and prosecutors useful advice on how to handle cases involving the use of the internet for terrorist goals in the criminal justice system.

By implementing the right controls and informing your friends and family when known hazards exist, you can improve your chances of avoiding cyberterrorism. The following list shows ways in which individuals and businesses can defend against cyberterrorism:

- Use strong passwords. Since software exists that can quickly guess thousands of passwords, a difficult password is one that is likely to be secure. Observe recommended practices for passwords by changing them frequently and avoiding using the same one for multiple logins.

- Follow cybersecurity news to stay current on industry developments and government alerts. Knowing the most recent threats might help you get ready for potential terrorist activities.

- Create a culture of cyber awareness by requiring all staff members to participate in ongoing training on cybersecurity. Emphasize the need to be watchful and alert to any suspicious activity.

- Check out every third-party vendor because a company's third-party vendors ultimately determine how secure the company is online. Before entering into any agreements or conducting any business, companies should require vendor openness regarding their cybersecurity policies.

The ongoing efforts to educate professionals and internet users, to raise the culture of safety in cyberspace, and to implement deftly designed and continuously adaptive technological, organizational, and regulatory measures may have an impact on the prevention of cyberterrorism, the reduction of risks to an acceptable level, and ultimately maintain the progress of civilization in cyberspace, not its destruction.

Summary

In the age of information technology, terrorism can be divided into three categories: conventional terrorism, where traditional weapons (such as explosives and guns) are used to physically harm resources and people; techno terrorism, where traditional weapons are used to harm infrastructure and cause damage online; and cyberterrorism, where new weapons (such as malicious software, electromagnetic and microwave weapons) are used. Security agencies that are in charge of looking into terrorism, including cyberterrorism, must be on guard due to the prevalence of cyberterrorism and its phenomenon. This includes making sure that there is enough funding for staffing, tools, and training, as well as urging people to be alert and report any suspicious activity. The following chapter discusses ways in which law enforcement and the private sector combat crime on the Dark Web.

Part 3: Efforts to Combat Crimes on the Dark Web

The objective of *Part 3* is to help the reader to understand the various methods used by law enforcement, the private sector, and technology companies to combat crimes on the Dark Web. Additionally, this part proposes a system to combat crimes on the Dark Web more effectively.

This part has the following chapters:

- *Chapter 7, Efforts for Combating Crime on the Dark Web*
- *Chapter 8, System for Combating Crime on the Dark Web*
- *Chapter 9, Discussion and Evaluation*

7
Efforts for Combating Crime on the Dark Web

Some people claim that the Dark Web supports fundamental rights including *free speech*, *privacy*, and *anonymity*. On the other hand, governmental organizations and prosecutors worry that it is a sanctuary for severe illicit activity. Policing this part of the internet entails focusing on particular web behaviors that are regarded as illicit or subject to internet censorship. Police normally utilize the suspect's **Internet Protocol** (**IP**) address when looking into internet suspects, but since Dark Web technologies create anonymity, this becomes extremely difficult. As a result, law enforcement has used a variety of alternative strategies to track down and detain those using the Dark Web for illicit purposes. **Open Source Intelligence** (**OSINT**) is a method of data gathering and is used to legally collect data from public sources. Officers can use Dark Web-specific OSINT technologies to locate titbits of knowledge that will help them learn more about interactions occurring on the Dark Web.

This chapter will cover the following topics:

- Law enforcement techniques
- Tools for combating crime on the Dark Web
- Recommendations
- General needs and challenges

Law enforcement techniques

It was revealed in 2015 that Interpol provides a special Dark Web training course with technical details on TOR, cybersecurity, and practice darknet market takedowns. The UK's National Crime Agency and GCHQ announced the establishment of a *joint operations cell* to concentrate on cybercrime in October 2013. This squad was given the responsibility of combating child exploitation on the Dark Web as well as other cybercrimes in November 2015. Researchers, law enforcement, and policymakers are becoming increasingly interested in the Dark Web since it is characterized by the unknown, according to a comprehensive analysis of it published by the Congressional Research Service in March 2017. Reports in August 2017 claimed that *where possible and required*, cybersecurity companies that monitor and study the Dark Web on behalf of banks and retailers often communicate their findings with the FBI and other law enforcement agencies on illicit content.

The anonymity associated with Dark Web activities makes it difficult for investigators to assemble the evidence puzzle and prosecute criminals. Also, investigators often overlook significant evidence. This evidence may include encryption keys, Dark Web addresses, or cryptocurrency wallets. Lack of knowledge about the Dark Web and how criminals take advantage of it is a crucial problem and can, in some cases, slow down investigation processes (*Goodison et al., 2019*).

Data about the effectiveness of investigating Dark Web crime cases shows that this kind of crime is still a new and developing concept for jurisdictions and institutions (*Guzman, 2019*). Before the advent of advanced processing software, crime investigations were limited to leads related to reports, events, and tangential evidence connected to other crimes. Traditional police work could not adequately identify the diverse networks of a larger crime gang that had operations spanning numerous cities or countries. With the introduction of new sophisticated tools, law enforcement is able to generate tactical intelligence from large data, as well as efficiently document the operations of a crime gang (*Meyer* and *Shelley, 2020*). Part of this section will focus on answering the following two questions:

- What kinds of methods or tactics should the police be prohibited from using when fighting crime on the Dark Web?
- What considerations should guide police actions regarding using methods that may not be prohibited but are nevertheless seriously harmful?

Furthermore, this chapter discusses how law enforcement agencies should approach both the task of weighing the harms and benefits of operations on the Dark Web and that of explaining and justifying these kinds of operations to the public. Additionally, law enforcement agents, cybersecurity consultants, academic researchers, and civil rights advocates agree that research on improving information sharing is likely to have the greatest impact on fighting crime on the Dark Web (*Meyer* and *Shelley, 2020*).

Moreover, law enforcement should consider the following measures (if possible):

1. Multi-sector collaboration between various law enforcement and private sector agencies across the world.

2. Propose stricter laws to regulate the Dark Web.

3. Implement harsher punishments for criminals operating on the Dark Web.

These measures could potentially create a situation where operating on the Dark Web is of high risk (for criminals). As a result, criminals would be incentivized to operate more on the Surface Web or other places, where they are more easily identifiable. This kind of approach makes crimes easier to investigate and prosecute, as it disrupts criminals' organized networks and deters them from hiding on the Dark Web. The following sections show some techniques and methods law enforcement uses to detect and capture criminals on the Dark Web.

Sting operations

The Dark Web's anonymity allows police agents to conduct surveillance leaving almost no traces. Law enforcement agencies engage in a variety of online policing strategies to fight crime, though some of these strategies present a series of inadequacies and ethical dilemmas (*Zeid*, *Moubarak*, and *Bassil*, *2020*). By creating pseudo-personas, police agents access illicit Dark Web sites pretending to be fellow offenders or victims with the purpose of luring potential offenders into committing a crime. This kind of surveillance is also known as a **sting** operation and is frequently used to fight the commercial sexual exploitation of children. Online sting operations resemble traditional sting operations. By definition, sting operations consist of four components (*Reid* and *Fox*, *2020*):

- An enticement or opportunity to commit a crime, either created or exploited by law enforcement

- A targeted likely offender, or a group of offenders for a particular type of crime

- An undercover police officer, or some form of deception

- A *gotcha* climax when the forensic operation ends with arrests

Regarding the aforementioned, law enforcement agencies should create supplementary (detailed) guidance for authorized and covert police officers conducting operations aiming at disrupting crime on the Dark Web. This practice can ensure that the operations are carried out in ways that are necessary and proportionate. Additionally, the effectiveness of tactics used by the police should be monitored systematically in order to create the kind of evidence base on which better practices could be developed. Law enforcement agencies should be as transparent as possible concerning the outcomes of operations and how these constitute effectiveness. Also, efforts should be made to develop evaluation techniques that will be able to measure the currently undervalued disruption effects of methods and operations. Although covert operations are an important tool for law enforcement, criminals' understanding of these operations may preclude them from providing a long-term solution to the issue of crime on the Dark Web.

Honeypot traps

A few directions could assist in better understanding and addressing crime on the Dark Web. Arguably the most straightforward involves an increased amount of attention being placed on websites that promote crime—for instance, understanding whether shutting down sites with a large footprint in online sex trafficking effectively combats this kind of crime or simply shifts it to other locations. Research suggests that shutting down such websites does not consider how the visibility of sex trafficking has encouraged collaborative efforts between governments and other organizations (*Musto and Boyd, 2014*). Suppose law enforcement allows sex trafficking sites to stay active for more extended periods of time. In this case, it is possible that the police can better assist trafficked victims and identify patterns of how these criminal gangs operate.

An example of how keeping trafficking sites active can better assist investigations is the use of **honeypot traps**. A honeypot trap is a cybersecurity method aimed, among other strategies, at deceiving cybercriminals. These traps are sites that purport to be related to illegal activity but, in fact, are set up by police with the purpose of identifying and capturing potential offenders (*Zeid, Moubarak, and Bassil, 2020*). An instance of a honeypot trap is *Operation Pacifier*. This operation involved the FBI hijacking the pedophile site *Playpen* (in 2015) and continuing to serve content. 2 weeks after hacking the Playpen website, FBI agents used their position to pull off aggressive surveillance on the website's users. During that time, the FBI used a malware-based technique to hack into the users' browsers, uncovering IP addresses and other relevant information. The operation produced the following results (*FBI, 2017*):

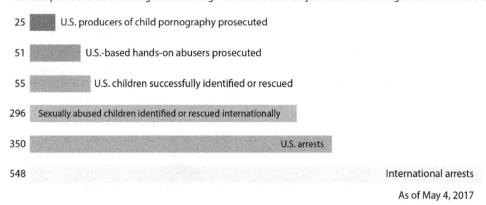

'Playpen' by the Numbers

The ongoing investigation of the Playpen child pornography website and its members led to its takedown in 2015 and has produced the following results through continued efforts by law enforcement agencies around the world:

25   U.S. producers of child pornography prosecuted

51   U.S.-based hands-on abusers prosecuted

55   U.S. children successfully identified or rescued

296   Sexually abused children identified or rescued internationally

350   U.S. arrests

548   International arrests

As of May 4, 2017

Figure 7.1 – Playpen by numbers

The Playpen operation represents one of the FBI's most successful efforts in combating crime on the Dark Web. This operation has opened new avenues for international cooperation to prosecute criminals. However, there are some serious issues regarding the methods used by the FBI. Although the idea of using *honeypot traps* to stop traffickers from acting on the Dark Web is intriguing, there are significant ethical issues with such strategies. The fact that many people view honeypot traps as a type of entrapment and a breach of civil liberties is a major cause for concern. Those involved in these techniques claimed that the purpose of the traps is to lessen the sense of freedom and anonymity and to instill doubt in offenders' minds (*Zeid*, *Moubarak*, and *Bassil*, *2020*).

Furthermore, law enforcement must continue to cooperate with payment companies to limit access to Dark Web child sexual exploitation material, especially live streaming child abuse. The establishment of the **European Financial Coalition** (**EFC**) against commercial sexual exploitation of children online is one example of such an attempt. This group brings together significant players from the commercial sector, law enforcement, and civil society to fight child sex trafficking on the Dark Web. To take advantage of the payment methods that are being used in illegitimate online transactions, members of the EFC must work together. Additionally, tackling Dark Web sex trafficking requires cooperation between governments, local communities, academia, and ex-trafficked victims. Also, support to individuals with a sexual interest in children can help to reduce the severity of the problem. A good initiative in this regard is the `helplinks.eu` website (*Figure 7.2*), which provides several links for help and prevention in various countries worldwide (*Europol*, *2018*):

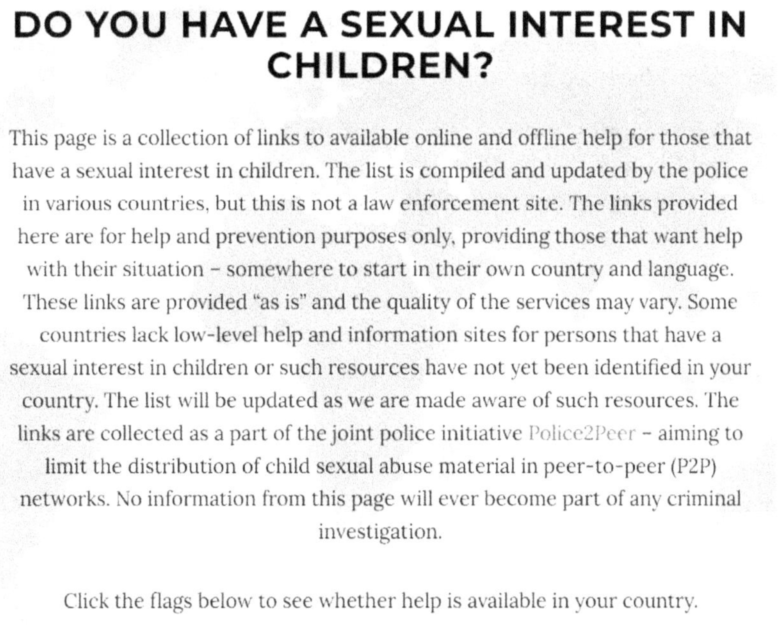

DO YOU HAVE A SEXUAL INTEREST IN CHILDREN?

This page is a collection of links to available online and offline help for those that have a sexual interest in children. The list is compiled and updated by the police in various countries, but this is not a law enforcement site. The links provided here are for help and prevention purposes only, providing those that want help with their situation – somewhere to start in their own country and language. These links are provided "as is" and the quality of the services may vary. Some countries lack low-level help and information sites for persons that have a sexual interest in children or such resources have not yet been identified in your country. The list will be updated as we are made aware of such resources. The links are collected as a part of the joint police initiative Police2Peer – aiming to limit the distribution of child sexual abuse material in peer-to-peer (P2P) networks. No information from this page will ever become part of any criminal investigation.

Click the flags below to see whether help is available in your country.

Figure 7.2 – helplinks.eu website

For those who are aware that their sexual interest in minors is unhealthy and want to take action, `helplinks.eu` is a free information source. Links are gathered by the police in the nations where the services are located, but there is no relationship between the services and law enforcement, and they do not communicate with or share information with the police. It may be possible to stop child abuse and/or the ownership or dissemination of photographs that depict such abuse by seeking therapy for a sexual interest in children.

Tools for combating crime on the Dark Web

Access to the Dark Web is necessary for law enforcement organizations to track criminals' digital traces and learn more about their networks, transactions, and accomplices. However, Dark Web scanning to gather and evaluate massive data from Dark Web markets, forums, blogs, online message boards, and social media is time-consuming and difficult. Therefore, in order to detect and discover connections between offenders and different identities, investigators and analysts need OSINT technologies for Dark Web scanning. For useful insights, the outcomes of the examined OSINT data sources must be displayed in graphs and maps. To put it another way, a top-notch Dark Web scanning service is required.

In order to solve and prevent crimes such as cyber threats, investigators and analysts use Dark Web monitoring technologies to identify threat actors, track the Bitcoin money trail, and map links between threat actors, their affiliates, and group members. Tools for monitoring the Dark Web can also be used to identify and stop insider threats. Such internet monitoring software can look for specific assets (such as research papers, private memos, or drafts of patents) or specific organizations (such as banks or research labs) that are directly mentioned in order to determine whether someone is being targeted or whether a breach may have occurred.

Since many Dark Web forums and message boards are in different languages, including English, Arabic, Russian, and Chinese, the top Dark Web monitoring systems employ clever algorithms, particularly **natural language processing** (**NLP**). Language limitations can be surmounted while gathering and evaluating intelligence with the use of a Dark Web scanning service. In addition to digital forensics and other technologies often used to investigate and prevent crimes such as cyber threats, law enforcement and security organizations need the best Dark Web monitoring services on the market. Internet surveillance tools give law enforcement personnel a proactive, cutting-edge way to track down heinous Dark Web activity, identify it, and put a stop to it.

Traffic confirmation attack

Internet communication traffic is usually encrypted in order to hide its contents. However, encrypted traffic is vulnerable to traffic analysis since it does not hide the metadata of the packets—that is, the time a packet was sent or received, and the packet's size. A traffic confirmation attack works by observing both ends of a communication channel and trying to find patterns in the traffic to match incoming and outgoing data (*Johnson et al., 2013*).

In the case of the TOR network, a traffic confirmation attack is possible when police take control of the relays on both ends of a TOR circuit. By doing this, the police can compare traffic timing, volume, and other characteristics, and eventually determine that the two relays are indeed in the same circuit. If the circuit's first relay knows the user's IP address, and the last relay in the circuit knows the destination the user is accessing, then law enforcement can deanonymize the user and reveal their identity (*TOR Project Blog, 2014*). The following diagram shows a clear representation of how a TOR traffic confirmation attack works (*Green, 2014*). SIGINT (signals intelligence) is information gathered by collecting and analyzing the electronic signals of a given target (*Whatls, 2021*):

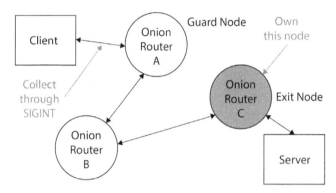

Figure 7.3 – Traffic confirmation attack on the TOR network

On July 4, 2014, the TOR project team found a group of relays that were trying to deanonymize users. They seem to have targeted users or operators of TOR hidden services. To conduct traffic confirmation attacks, the assault entailed altering TOR protocol headers. According to reports, the FBI gave instructions to a *university-based research institute* to identify criminal suspects on the so-called Dark Web. Circumstantial evidence suggested that the organization was Carnegie Mellon University (US) and, specifically, the Software Engineering department. Following a media frenzy, the university issued a press release that was extremely carefully written and suggested that it had received a subpoena for the IP addresses it had collected throughout its investigation.

OSINT

Techniques such as OSINT and a proper understanding of how the Dark Web works are crucial steps in combating crime and abuse in this hidden part of the internet. OSINT is derived from information and data that the general public can access. Collecting and possessing vast amounts of data in a timely manner is not humanly possible without the aid of OSINT tools (*Sharma, Breeden*, and *Fruhlinger, 2021*). By following the OSINT approach and applying a number of detection algorithms, law enforcement can uncover potential avenues for investigating Dark Web crime more effectively.

Openly available tools, such as NodeXL and Gephi3, facilitate both network analysis as well as network visualization (*Akhgar, Bayerl,* and *Sampson, 2017*). The OSINT approach can be an excellent method for gathering important information about the criminality that occurs on the Dark Web and prosecuting criminals easier. The following diagram shows OSINT's life cycle (*Talaviya, 2019*):

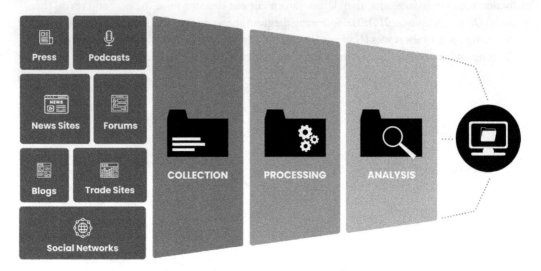

Figure 7.4 – OSINT's life cycle

The MEMEX project

Nowadays, web searches use a centralized, one-size-fits-all approach that crawls the internet with the same tools for all queries. Although this model has been widely successful commercially, it seems not to work well for governmental use cases. In order to overcome this challenge, **DARPA**, also known as the **Defense Advanced Research Projects Agency**, launched the MEMEX project in September 2014. MEMEX is a highly sophisticated search tool that goes beyond the realm of Google, Bing, and Yahoo. The following screenshot shows some of the most significant domains that the MEMEX team is working on (*JPL MEMEX, 2021*):

GeoInformatics in Human Trafficking

Collects data and information around victims of human trafficking with geospatial informatics capabilities

Facial Recognition

Manages photos of potential terrorists and finds other places they exist on the web

Material Research

Collect and analyzes data from research papers to create shared knowledge around an issue or topic

Court Citations

Crawls the web for court documents to help identify human traffickers

Figure 7.5 – MEMEX's domains

The MEMEX project aims to move to the next level: the art of content indexing and web searching. Over the years, the MEMEX team has released new tools that enable the quick and thorough organization of the internet's content. This has led to more comprehensive and relevant domain-specific indexing and domain-specific searching capabilities (*Darpa.mil, 2021*). One of MEMEX's main goals is to shine a light on the Dark Web and uncover behavioral tactics and relationships that can help law enforcement disrupt large human trafficking gangs (*Zetter, 2015*).

The MEMEX project has been in the works for years and is being developed by 17 different contractor teams across the world. Conventional search engines, such as Google and Bing, show results based on popularity and ranking and are only able to index approximately 5 percent of the World Wide Web. On the contrary, MEMEX is able to scrape web pages that get ignored by commercial engines, as well as to show hidden sites on the Dark Web. MEMEX's creators do not want just to index web content about previously undiscovered sites. They aim to use automated methods in order to identify behavioral patterns of how human traffickers operate on the Dark Web (*Zetter, 2015*). The inventor of MEMEX, Chris White, said that this tool could revolutionize law enforcement investigations and give a new positive perspective on combating human trafficking on the Dark Web (*CBS News, 2015*).

According to reports, on numerous occasions, MEMEX's **artificial intelligence** (**AI**) has helped several police investigations all over the world. With the aid of MEMEX tools, law enforcement is now able to quickly strengthen newly discovered cases and construct sex trafficking investigations from hazy leads. These technologies—such as TellFinder (created by MEMEX contributor Uncharted Software) for indexing, summarizing, and querying sex ad data—have been used, for instance, to find more minor victims from information in a single online prostitution advertisement.

Recommendations

Undercover web investigations are one tactic that law enforcement agencies all over the world frequently use. Enforcement officers have used investigation chat rooms and other **peer-to-peer** (**P2P**) networks to pose as criminals or participants in illegal activity during such investigations. The following are some recommendations that will help to mitigate crime on the Dark Web:

- **Crime identification**: Line officers need to become educated on the sorts and extent of illegal activity taking place on the Dark Web. A good initiative is new state task teams that may share information on the Dark Web among organizations and jurisdictions.

- **Privacy protection**: The need for advice from federal partners on how to handle privacy concerns during investigations. There is a need for research to determine how much privacy people would be willing to give up in exchange for security.

- **Suspect identifications**: Officers responding to criminal activity need to learn to identify elements such as login information that may be used to connect offenders to Dark Web sites.

- **Evidence identification, access, and preservation**: Law enforcement may find it challenging to compile pertinent technical data and translate it into evidence that members of the general public who serve on juries that determine whether or not people accused of Dark Web violations are guilty or innocent can understand. The evidential conundrum is a result of the increasing volume of data, the complexity of the forms, and the need for cross-jurisdictional cooperation. In light of the difficulties posed by the encryption and anonymity features of the software used on the Dark Web, the delegates advised law enforcement to employ the best standards, instruments, and techniques available to acquire evidence. To that aim, encouraging the adoption of standards for new techniques used to gather evidence from the Dark Web was identified as a high priority.

As cybercriminals become increasingly tech-savvy, it is crucial for law enforcement to keep up with the new trends and activities related to crime on the Dark Web. The US **National Institute of Justice** (**NIJ**) created a guide with high-level recommendations for conducting forensic investigations on the Dark Web. The guide was produced with the help of experts from state, federal, and local agencies, civil rights advocates, and academic researchers (*US National Institute of Justice, 2020*). Here are some significant points from this guide, including crucial Dark Web challenges:

- **Training**: Train investigators and officers to spot relevant Dark Web evidence.

- **Partnerships**: Build cross-jurisdictional partnerships.

- **New forensic tools**: Develop new forensic tools for collecting Dark Web evidence on computers and mobiles.

- **Information sharing**: Improve information sharing among agencies, both on a domestic and an international level.

- **New structures for cooperation**: Examine the advantages of building cross-organizational structures for cooperation.

- **New laws for package inspection**: Research methods to modernize laws related to the inspection of packages shipped by mail or other services.

- **Hardening the device identification for law enforcement units**: **Trusted Platform Module (TPM)** is put inside modern IT systems to grant security-by-design features for users. It can be leveraged to identify internet users and make it harder to anonymize and hide from law enforcement. Blockchain can be used as an immutable ledger to track devices from the manufacturer to the end user. New systems unique to investigators can pave the way to combating crime on the Dark Web.

- **Research on crime connections**: To assist law enforcement authorities in identifying and combating both highly visible traditional crime and less obvious criminality on the Dark Web, research the increasingly interrelated nature of traditional crime.

In recent years, law enforcement agencies all over the world have started to rely on the use of hacking to track down online criminals who operate in anonymity. Internet thieves are now better protected because of the growth of the Dark Web, which obscures digital footprints left by third parties, leaving traditional surveillance measures obsolete. Enforcement agencies have started implementing hacking techniques that run surveillance software over the internet to directly access and control criminals' computers in order to circumvent Dark Web defenses.

General needs and challenges

Even while it may appear that the Dark Web is untraceable, there is some chance of uncovering criminals using it. In other words, no crime is perfect, and criminals frequently make mistakes or leave unintentional clues:

- **Rapid changes in the volume of use**: Although there is evidence of a constant increase in Dark Web activity, law enforcement lacks the quantitative information necessary to respond to these activities effectively.

- **Globalization**: Activity on the Dark Web transcends regional, governmental, and international barriers. Because the Dark Web spans jurisdictions, it is crucial that investigators from different agencies work together. Participants warned that *Dark Web operators would be emboldened by the lack of enforcement to conduct more unlawful activities via the Dark Web* if agencies shun the Dark Web due to its cross-jurisdictional character.

- **The need to demystify the Dark Web**: Some law enforcement participants expressed worry that, should they take action against Dark Web interests, harmful online users would retaliate against them and their departments. The research noted that there was *a need to demystify the Dark Web* for law enforcement, stating that *law enforcement is expected to respond without comprehensive information regarding what works and what is required to solve these Dark Web difficulties*. Participants indicated that police instructors may emphasize the similarities between standard investigations and *plain old police work*, or Dark Web investigations.

- **Command buy-in for additional training**: Participants emphasized the importance of persuading law enforcement command staff to begin Dark Web training and investigations. Command buy-in may be required in order to make financial and training time commitments.

- **Training**: There is a requirement for two different types of training:

  - Courses for line officers to gain a basic understanding of digital evidence discovered on the spot

  - Targeted training on the preservation of evidence as well as sophisticated instruction on the techniques employed by criminals on the Dark Web is recommended for specialist units

Law enforcement authorities identified priority needs for investigating criminal activity on the Dark Web:

- Educating state and local officials about the Dark Web.

- Establishing cross-jurisdictional alliances between agencies.

- Providing more and better training to better prepare police officers to recognize Dark Web activity and evidence.

- Providing superior knowledge of Dark Web techniques and operations to special investigating groups. Due to the Dark Web's secrecy, many state and local law enforcement authorities are generally ignorant of its presence and its potential to fuel crime in their areas.

Summary

Investigators can explore the Dark Web using advanced systems by gathering, examining, and keeping track of data in a tactical timeframe. The internet surveillance software and Dark Web monitoring instruments on this cutting-edge web intelligence platform are intended to speed up web investigation procedures. The powerful web engine analyzes gathered data using sophisticated AI algorithms and provides in-depth insights in real time. A cybercrime inquiry can also be started by investigators using any minor piece of digital forensics data, such as a suspect's identity, location, IP address, or image, thanks to Dark Web monitoring services. Law enforcement and governmental agencies will be able to scour and monitor the Dark Web with sophisticated technologies in order to gather and analyze pertinent big data that will provide streamlined, automated insights for prompt action. The next chapter discusses the proposal of a system to combat crime on the Dark Web more effectively.

System for Combating Crime on the Dark Web

The cryptographic and anonymity features of the Dark Web create severe difficulties for law enforcement agencies to investigate, monitor, control, prosecute, and prevent a range of criminal events. This chapter describes the steps for developing an efficient system for preventing/mitigating crime on the Dark Web. The system could be utilized as a real-life paradigm by law enforcement, cybersecurity researchers, and local police agencies that will help them to study and combat crimes on the Dark Web.

In this chapter, we will cover the following topics:

- Problem identification

- Problem handling

- The feasibility of creating a universal system

- Steps to creating a system

- Final system proposal

- Centralized system design—**International Data Hub (IDH)**

Problem identification

Through the extensive literature examination, several problems regarding efforts of combating crimes on the Dark Web have been identified. Currently, there are numerous entities/tools/methods that are used to combat these kinds of crimes, such as the MEMEX project, traffic confirmation attacks, Oracle's advanced technology, and so on. However, all these entities are not succinctly in line with one another. This means that entity A may have different information than entity B and entity C. There is a lack of a consolidated platform where investigators can put all this information together, process it, and interact with it. Another significant issue is the lack of real-time insights. This kind of insight can help investigators to visualize data and take prompt actions to help crime victims. Based on all the aforementioned, this research has concluded that the ultimate goal of the system is the following:

- Preventing Dark Web-related crimes

- Prompt identification and prosecution of criminals

- Helping crime victims and their families

- Providing awareness among the public about how crimes can be mitigated

Problem handling

The system aims to create a fully integrated platform to face the problem of crimes on the Dark Web. A way to handle the problem is prevention, across and throughout all industries, building communities resilient to crimes. Taking the decentralized databases and forcing them into a single source of an independent database can be a significant step forward. This provides one centralized, secure place for all data. The system's purpose is to develop a platform that gets real-time information and then, by using advanced cloud software, integrate this information into an autonomous data warehouse. Through radical information sharing and collaboration, the system aims to build a global picture of crime hotspots/trends and empower individuals, organizations, and law enforcement agencies in making more informed decisions.

The feasibility of creating a universal system

The analysis of the literature suggests that the current methods of combating crimes on the Dark Web are not adequate for the needs of digital forensics' fast-paced and quick-changing environment. One of the most significant problems of modern law enforcement investigations is that they lack adequate efficiency. This is evidenced by the fact that this kind of crime continues to be a very serious problem for societies all over the world. To maintain a reliable forensic platform, it is necessary to figure out the problem or area of opportunity. This is where systems come in—they help to comprehend the problem in a new way. Before prototyping, testing, and launching, the problem should be framed in an approachable way (*Conley, 2016*).

The digital forensics field has been expanding dramatically and continues to advance quickly. The challenge with the system aiming to propose is to present evidence with a reliable method in order to meet all current and future requirements. This section will concentrate on two topics:

- Existing models used by investigators

- The choice of the most appropriate approach for the system

The following diagram shows the simplest digital forensics model in existence, developed by the **National Institute of Standards and Technology (NIST)** in 2006 (*Davies* and *Smith, 2019*):

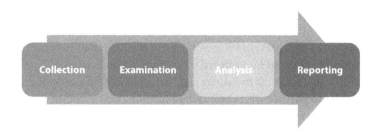

Figure 8.1 – NIST's forensic model

The process of doing a digital forensic investigation involves the following (*NIST, 2006*):

- **Collection**: This is the procedure of identifying any potential sources of data relevant to an incident and then accurately labeling and recording that data. Subsequently, the data located in these sources must be acquired while preserving the integrity of the sources.

- **Examination**: This phase involves assessing the data acquired from the previous procedure and extracting data that is relevant to the incident while preserving the data's integrity and validity.

- **Analysis**: This phase has to do with the study of the information extracted by the examination phase. It can only be done by using legal/justifiable methods, procedures, and techniques.

- **Reporting**: This phase involves the process of presenting, in a structured manner, the methods, procedures, and tools used in the previous phases. Additionally, the reporting process provides recommendations for improvement to the tools, policies, and other aspects of the forensic process.

Cybersecurity functions include protection, detection, response, and investigation. Digital forensic systems are essential because they can help in mitigating damages and maturing future prevention approaches. Nowadays, investigating Dark Web crimes has evolved more than ever, combining intelligent tools and sophisticated forensic processes. Digital forensic processes have been able to aid investigations by identifying and analyzing the facts related to a crime incident. Additionally, automatic processes would allow for bigger volumes of evidence to be processed more intelligently and accurately (*Dimitriadis, Ivezic, Kulvatunyou*, and *Mavridis, 2020*). The following list describes some characteristics of traditional digital forensic systems (*Davies* and *Smith, 2019*):

- Provide a clear definition of standard technological terms

- Allow individuals to train at the same level of knowledge and expertise

- Ensure that evidence is not misused or mishandled

- Give confidence to the system consumer

- Ensure that the industry has integrity

- Update systems regularly to keep pace with new trends

Steps to creating a system

This research has concluded that prevention may be more effective than investigating individual crime incidents themselves. This can be achieved by creating an international database/system to facilitate information sharing (across all industries and sectors) about crimes on the Dark Web. This international system aims to partner with various organizations and agencies, including financial institutions, international law enforcement, non-governmental agencies, the UN, local and federal police authorities, the public, and many others.

By using advanced cognitive technologies, the proposed centralized system will focus on facilitating information sharing easily and quickly and combining several datasets in one secure database. Additionally, **artificial intelligence (AI)** can play a significant role and help to analyze and process large volumes of data quickly, while ensuring the data's security and integrity. Additionally, predictive policing can look at vast data on crimes in a certain area and make predictions about when and where crimes will happen in the short and long term.

By thoroughly examining the literature, three entities have been identified that can play a vital role in combating crimes on the Dark Web. These entities are the following:

- **Law enforcement**: This term describes some members of the government who are responsible for enforcing laws, managing public safety, and maintaining public order. The term *law enforcement* includes agencies such as the FBI, Europol, Interpol, CIA, and the British Secret Intelligence Services (*Post, 2021*).

- **Private sector**: This term refers to the part of society that is not controlled by the government. It includes private banks, for-profit businesses, corporations, charities, non-government agencies, and many others (*Gocardless, 2021*).

- **Community**: This term mainly refers to ordinary people living in cities, suburban areas, and villages. It may also include the municipal police, county sheriff's departments, and local law enforcement agencies (*Study.com, 2021*).

Developing an information-sharing system will help to achieve the following:

- Streamline information sharing between all the involved parties

- Create better crime investigation practices

- Allow each entity to understand the requirements, limitations, and procedures related to information sharing

- Provide the opportunity to address some of the challenges that emerge in regard to sharing information across partners and disciplines

Information sharing among the entities mentioned earlier is essential to establish solid partnerships and address the issues of crimes on the Dark Web. A successful collaborative approach to identifying, investigating, and prosecuting criminals will require information to be shared between partners about cases, victims, and traffickers. By creating an IDH, the police can support and engage with a victim, as well as disrupt large well-organized crime organizations. The data collected by this hub will help to identify trends and develop appropriate, data-driven, well-informed forensic models. Based on all the aforementioned, an initial design for the system has been created. The following screenshot shows the three entities sharing information with the IDH:

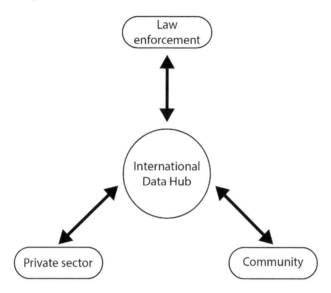

Figure 8.2 – Initial system design

It has been recognized that only when everybody comes together, practical solutions that break the cycle of crimes on the Dark Web can be created. Through extensively researching and reviewing the literature, numerous tools/methods/techniques that are being used to combat Dark Web crimes have been identified. All these tools belong to the three entities that were mentioned previously: 1) **law enforcement**, 2) **the private sector**, and 3) **the community**. In the following table, all the tools/methods/techniques are categorized based on the three entities:

Entities	Tools/Methods/Techniques
Law enforcement	MEMEX project Traffic confirmation attack Intelligence-led policing Predictive analytics Honeypot traps Sting operations
Private sector	Oracle's advanced technology Pipl Search Private technology companies Banks and fintech OSINT Project Arachnid MFScope
Community	Stop child abuse—trace an object

Figure 8.3 – Categorization of tools based on the three main entities

Final system proposal

The previous sections outlined several important factors to consider when creating a digital forensics system. The aim of this section is to merge all the aforementioned to compile a reasonably complete platform. All the entities/tools/methods/techniques mentioned in earlier sections will be incorporated into this system. The system's goal is to establish a clear picture of the steps that should be followed when investigating Dark Web crime cases. The proposed system is scalable and can be easily expanded in the future, and include any necessary additional phases.

Police and community stakeholders must cooperate effectively by delegating tasks, allocating resources, and making decisions jointly. Therefore, collaboration entails coordinated actions with shared responsibility and decision-making rather than just outreach or information sharing. Addressing a problem demands proactive cooperation between the police and the community in order to uncover underlying issues that can be resolved to eradicate the root causes of crime. The following diagram shows a clear representation of the final system proposal:

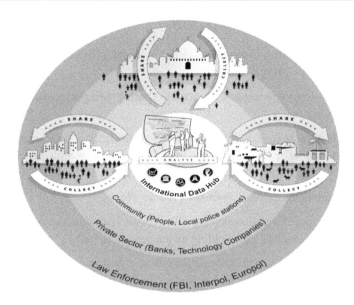

Figure 8.4 – Final system proposal

The system design shown in *Figure 8.4* focuses on combating crimes on the Dark Web by engaging in a positive and collaborative way with law enforcement, the private sector, and the community. This system aims to encourage greater sharing and better collaboration and fight crimes by cooperating with various entities. The system can be the basis for combating crimes on the Dark Web more effectively. Through the availability of data, the system's goal is to make crimes and exploitation highly transparent. In this way, every party, in every sector, can see the data in its own context and then make a decision on how it engages with it.

Centralized system design – IDH

The following points provide a list of items that anti-crime law enforcement should consider when developing an information-sharing system. This list can be used as an advanced guide for the development of a robust and reliable system. While it is not compulsory to include all items, it is essential that law enforcement members discuss and agree on what must be included and what not. The following is a list of what is needed for the IDH:

- **Introduction to the IDH:**
    - The rationale for the information-sharing system
    - Individuals who helped in designing the system (including representatives from the private sector, law enforcement, prosecution, and trafficking victims' support services)
    - Schedule periodic updates and reviews of the system

- **Specific information to be shared in the IDH:**

  - Where the information is being stored at the moment. (For example, is the information safely maintained in a specific database?)

  - Trafficking the victim's permission in regard to sharing their personal data, records, type of trafficking, and so on.

  - Information that will be shared, in detail. (That is, will de-identified data*, sensitive information, or tips about victims be shared? If yes, what will be shared, by which entities, under what protection rules, and what role does confidentiality play?)

  - Who will be providing all this information and to whom?

  - Considerations for information sharing with broader law enforcement members. (That is, community members, non-case holding members, and so on.)

  - Circumstances in which various information will be shared and different exceptions that may preclude information sharing. (That is, understanding law enforcement partners that have privileged communication relationships with victims and are limited in what they can share.)

- **Requirements related to information sharing for the IDH:**

  - Requirements for information sharing as ordered by the local, state, and federal governments for each discipline participating in the system.

  - Steps that must be followed to meet all the requirements necessary for information sharing. (That is, how will the victims be informed of information shared about their cases? What kind of information will be shared with victims?)

  - Requirements for information sharing for each entity involved in the system. (That is, does a trafficking victim have to sign a release of information form, or are internal procedure approvals needed to share de-identified data*?)

  - Considerations related to information sharing for law enforcement to have in mind. (That is, which principles should be incorporated to make information sharing trauma-informed and victim-centered?)

  - Requirements for information sharing in case the victim is unable to be located. (That is, what steps should be followed to meet the requirements needed for information sharing?)

- **Processes related to information sharing for the IDH:**

  - Who is responsible for managing/collecting information? (That is, will there be a central department at each agency?)

  - How will confidentiality be maintained?

  - Where will the information be securely stored? (That is, who manages the IDH database, what steps should be followed in discovering a secure platform, and so on?)

- How will information be shared? (That is, does a data warehouse need to be created or purchased? If so, how will it be created and who will maintain it?)

- What is the process in case a breach of data occurs? (That is, who will be notified and how will people be held accountable?)

- Limitations to sharing information via the internet

De-identified data refers to data that is distributed without any information that would allow anyone to know to whom the data is connected. For example, data where names, addresses, birthdates, and other personal information are removed (HRPP, 2021).

Considerations for central intelligence hub system design

A centralized database management system, also known as a central computer database system, is a platform in which all of an organization's data is safely stored and managed in a single unit. This kind of platform is primarily used in governmental organizations, large companies, or private institutions to centralize their activities (*Mohammed* and *Maina, 2017*). A mainframe computer is an example of a centralized database management system. The basic function of such a system is to provide advanced facilities and give access to all the connected computers that fulfill all requirements requested by any single node (*Farnham, 2021*). The following are some of the main benefits of having an information-sharing centralized database:

- More accurate and reliable information

- It helps to make fast decisions and take prompt measures

- Find information quicker

- Eliminate redundant records about victims and offenders

- More effective collaboration

Furthermore, Dark Web criminal offenses are difficult to take to court for some of the same reasons that they are challenging to investigate. The frequent urge to rely on evidence collected abroad, as well as the potential for victims to be traumatized and intimidated, creates some difficult and complex challenges to the judiciary. Effective collaboration with victim assistance services, enhanced international judicial cooperation, and the development of more powerful witness protection measures must be part of any strategy in order to address these challenges (*United Nations Office on Drugs and Crime, 2020*).

Stakeholders planning to utilize advanced technologies to enhance the efforts of combating crimes on the Dark Web should take into consideration some significant aspects related to data privacy, ethics, and informed consent. Managing risks related to ethics, data privacy, and informed consent is hugely important in criminal cases because of the subjects of the data—the victims of exploitation. Victims' trauma could become even more severe if their personal data and story are accessed by irrelevant people. This would lead to an opposite effect than the one intended when developing the proposed IDH.

The IDH aims to enable law enforcement to combine both raw and processed data from multiple sources and formats in order to allow investigators to draw on an even richer pool of data. In this way, analysts will be better positioned to identify crime patterns, networks, and hotspots, as well as to focus on the right anti-crime resources in the right way. *The IDH should be hosted in a combination of centralized and cloud environments and utilize highly advanced technologies, such as AI, data visualization, machine learning (ML), and data analytics.*

Furthermore, the IDH can play a vital role in providing guidance, developing best practices, and securing uptake. In collaboration with global institutions, such as the FBI, Europol, and Interpol, the hub can become a proactive generator of self-regulation and good practice. Several recommendations have emerged from the discussion in this research. These recommendations are extracted from the text and reproduced as follows:

- The hub should adopt a targeted approach to policing crimes on the Dark Web, focusing on exposing, disrupting, and prosecuting criminals.

- The hub should put in place long-term and strategic provision of psychological, moral, and professional support for both officers and victims involved in operations.

- Research should be carried out to map law enforcement's reliance on the private sector. This will help to assess law enforcement's needs and to anticipate how this is likely to develop in the future. The outcomes of such research should be used to plan and invest, in a strategic way, in law enforcement's capabilities.

- The hub should ensure that means used by private enterprises are lawful and that evidence collected is admissible in court.

- In order to develop responsible and accountable practices, private sector companies offering services or tools for Dark Web crime investigations should develop, publish, and abide by digital forensics *codes of conduct*.

Hub control

This kind of hub brings together all of a company's controls, monitoring, and documentation into one platform to deliver a real-time management information system. Data is easily portable and scalable because it is stored in the same place. Also, the centralized database approach is cheaper than other types of databases as it requires less maintenance and power. All information in the centralized platform can be easily accessed from the same location and at the same time. The following screenshot describes some of the advanced features that a control hub/platform can have (*Deloitte, 2021*):

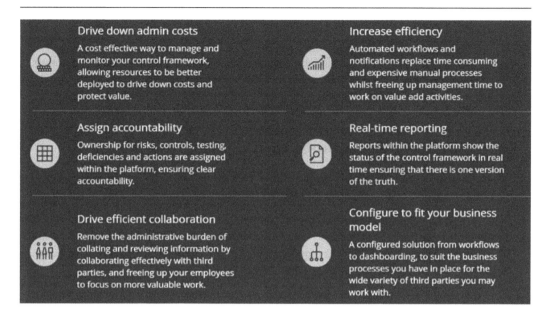

Figure 8.5 – Control hub advanced features

The following list describes some of the hub's primary goals:

- **Planning and implementation**: For the proposed IDH, defining a mission and establishing goals are insufficient. To accomplish and carry out its objective, the hub must act. Significant choices regarding employment, staffing, fundraising activities, and volunteer recruitment will be made by the hub's board. The board must also oversee and keep an eye on events and activities to make sure they continue to be in line with the hub's standards and objectives.

- **Financial matters**: Even though a project such as the proposed IDH isn't about making money, it nevertheless needs funding to run. The board is responsible for creating and approving the organization's annual budget as well as making sure that it abides by all applicable rules and laws.

- **Legal responsibilities**: Each board member has a fiduciary duty to the other board members and the hub. The board members have a fiduciary duty to act honestly. The board shouldn't take any actions that are against the hub's goals and objectives or indulge in self-dealing. Making sure the organization has a capable **chief executive officer** (**CEO**) and selecting a seasoned board that reflects a variety of interests in the community are two responsibilities that fall under this category.

Hub functions

In a conventional database system, data is stored in multiple files—for example, each trafficking victim's data may be stored in a separate file. On the other hand, a centralized database stores all the data in one file. This makes it more efficient to manage the data, and it is also easier to search the database, as they are all stored in the same place. In the case of the proposed IDH, all data gathered from the various entities will be stored in a combination of central and cloud databases. The following list describes some of the hub's main functions (*Powell et al., 2000*):

- **Distributed query processing**: The primary function of the proposed IDH is to provide suitable facilities and give access to all connected entities that fulfill all requirements requested by any single node.

- **Single central unit**: All the data will be stored in a single centralized and cloud database system. The computer system that fulfills the requirements of all the connected computers is known as a server, and other computers are defined as clients.

- **Transparency**: There is no irrelevant or duplicate data stored in the system. All connected computers have access to the central system for their query processing and requirements.

- **Scalable**: More computers can be added to this database management system. These computers are connected to the system through a network.

These databases will be easily accessible by authorized parties and categorized into various sections.

Summary

In the last few decades, pressure on organizations to maintain robust internal controls has increased dramatically. Audit committees, stakeholders, and boards are expecting management to provide not only transparency and accountability over internal controls but also real-time updates on their effectiveness. Additionally, with an ever-changing regulatory environment, increased remote working, and greater operational complexity, more pressure is put on already stretched management teams. Control hubs/central platforms have been designed to help alleviate this burden (*Chambers, 2021*). The next chapter provides a conclusion to the overall research.

Discussion and Evaluation

The Dark Web is a part of the internet that contains content that can only be accessed by using specialized browsers. Users must use specific software and configurations to browse this hidden part of the internet. By using the Dark Web, people worldwide can exchange messages and conduct business securely and anonymously without revealing recognizable information, such as IP addresses and locations. The Dark Web constitutes a small part of the Deep Web, the portion of the internet that is not indexed by traditional search engines. The Dark Web can be used for legitimate purposes as well as to conduct criminal activities related to weapons, fraud, drugs, child pornography, contract killings, terrorism, human trafficking, zoophilia, cannibalism, and many other offenses.

This chapter will cover the following topics:

- Structure of the research
- Overview of the research
- Final tips on how to use the Dark Web

Structure of the research

The research methodology is one of the most important aspects of any research process, including this book. It provides the basis upon which the research is procedurally undertaken, and it allows readers to evaluate the reliability and validity of the study. This chapter's main aim is to explain the methodology employed for the research. The adopted methodology is justified, along with the techniques, tools, and approaches that were used. Additionally, this chapter discusses the ethical dilemmas and concerns related to the book.

Research process

The research process is not a linear process in which researchers must complete step one before moving on to steps two or three. Depending on the familiarity with the topic and the challenges encountered along the way, it may be needed to rearrange or revisit these steps. The following diagram outlines a simple way in which research could be conducted (*Khoo, 2012*):

01 Research Question
Identify the gap in knowledge
Devise your research question

02 Research Objectives
Breakdown the research question into smaller objectives that will help you answer the main question.

03 Research Strategy
Identify what type of data (information) will be required to achieve your research objectives.

04 Methods for Data Collection
Decide which methods will be the most suitable for the type of data you want to collect. Be prepared to justify your choice.

05 Data Analysis Technique
It is important to think about which data analysis techniques you can use before your start collection data.

06 Expected Outcome
Think about what would be the final outcome of your project. What will be the possible contributions your work will make?

Figure 9.1 – A simple way of conducting the research

Defining a clear research question and objectives is a crucial step in any research process, especially for this book. On the one hand, the research question formulates a research problem that needs to be investigated. The scope of the research question is defined by the research objectives. On the other hand, the research objectives outline the specific steps that must be followed to answer the main question. Objectives define the following questions: *who, what, why, when,* and *how.*

The research question and objectives have helped in the following ways (*Farrugia et al., 2010*):

- Guided the literature search
- Guided the research design
- Guided the data collection process
- Guided the data analysis techniques
- Guided the writing-up of the data
- Restricted the research to be within boundaries

Philosophical paradigm

All researchers should be able to understand the application of various theories and practices used in the writing field. Before carrying out a research project, it is vital to identify the philosophical paradigm on which the research will be based. A philosophical paradigm is a system that involves the following (*Kivunja* and *Kuyini, 2017*):

1. Formulation of the problem

2. Choice of research strategy

3. Data collection

4. Processing

5. Analysis and testing

6. Evaluation

In this book, the philosophical paradigm has determined the research methods as well as how the data have been analyzed, tested, and evaluated.

Quantitative and qualitative research methods provide different outcomes and are often used in combination to get a full picture of a research problem. Both approaches are significant for gaining different kinds of knowledge. Due to the complexity of the area that is being investigated—that is, the Dark Web—and the importance of gathering reliable numerical and textual data about this topic, it has been decided to follow a mixture of the quantitative and qualitative methods. This approach has helped to produce *reliable data* by conducting interviews and creating questionnaires (both open- and closed-ended questions) and testing the proposed system. By following the process of interviews, the research objectives have been answered through this approach. The following list describes various ways the chosen approach has helped to answer the main question and objectives of this project:

- Enabled us to identify and understand components regarding the research objectives

- Enabled us to make an in-depth analysis of the subject (Dark Web)

- Enabled us to elaborate on the practical problem (crime on the Dark Web)

- Enabled us to understand the extent that existing research has advanced

- Enabled us to link theory with practice

- Enabled us to clarify relations, gaps, contradictions, and inconsistencies

- Enabled us to formulate statements and general conceptualizations

A combination of the quantitative and qualitative approaches is defined as the process of reviewing, analyzing, testing (by interviewing relevant participants), and critically evaluating scholarly articles, books, journals, and other high-quality sources relevant to a particular area of research (*Berland* and *Piot, 2013*). Data clusters are formed as outcomes of this procedure. This data is known as *primary data*. This approach helps the researcher cover a significant proportion of the research surface and justify that the data collected is accurate and reliable. Finally, the approach chosen acknowledges the work of previous researchers, and in so doing, assures the reader that the author's work has been well conceived (*Aristodemou* and *Tietze, 2018*).

Overview of the research

This chapter summarizes the results regarding each research objective and provides a concise and justifiable answer to the research question. Each research objective carried its own importance for the book and addressed a significant part of the research question. Also, this chapter discusses future work directions and how this project can contribute to the cybersecurity field. This book consisted of nine chapters, which are respectively divided into subsections. Each chapter served as a stepping stone toward answering the research objectives and research question.

The research approach chosen for this project was a combination of quantitative and qualitative methods. These methods have helped to get in-depth insights into Dark Web's ecosystem and produce reliable data clusters. These data clusters were formed by interviewing relevant people as well as by extensively reviewing, analyzing, and critically evaluating books, scholarly articles, journals, and other high-quality sources. Additionally, this approach has helped to investigate criminals' behavioral patterns with better accuracy and understand precisely how they operate on the Dark Web. The following text shows some significant advantages and disadvantages of the quantitative and qualitative approaches:

Advantages:

- They provided insights specific to the area of research
- They allowed for detail-oriented data to be collected
- They eliminated the potential for bias within the data
- They used fluid operational structures instead of rigid guidelines

Disadvantages:

- Research does not take place in its normal environment
- More time-consuming
- The researcher cannot generalize the findings
- Research can be expensive

In order to fulfill the research question, five research objectives were used to answer the research question. The research objectives are as follows:

1. Investigate the most common types of cybercrimes that take place on the Dark Web

Many types of cybercrimes take place on the Dark Web. The most common are drugs, distribution of weapons, fraud, counterfeit products, scams, and many others. In regard to cybercrimes such as human trafficking, the most common types are child pornography, modern slavery, sexual exploitation, organ trade, forced marriage, and others.

2. Investigate the tools used by criminals to access the Dark Web, as well as the methods they use to traffic and exploit humans

Human traffickers, by taking advantage of the anonymity that the Dark Web offers, use various tools in order to conduct their illegal activities. The most common ones that are used are *the TOR browser*, *I2P*, and *Freenet*. An extensive analysis of these tools was conducted in this research. By using advanced cryptographic mechanisms, the previously mentioned tools offer high anonymity to both the buyers and sellers of human trafficking-related services. In regard to the methods and components human traffickers use to conduct their illegal activities, the following three key elements have been identified:

1.   Grooming and recruitment of vulnerable victims

2.   Advertisements of illegal services

3.   Payment for business expenses and services

The aforementioned tools and methods were extensively reviewed and analyzed in the initial chapters.

3. Investigate the Dark Web's ecosystem and analyze how criminals operate within this hidden part of the internet – this will help to gain insights about them, such as their behavioral patterns, preferences, and the techniques they use

The Dark Web's ecosystem entails a variety of components, from methods on how to groom and exploit vulnerable humans to techniques on how to avoid law enforcement detection and prosecution. The process of finding crime-related services (for bad guys) starts with the setup of a Dark Web access tool such as TOR. Subsequently, the perpetrators find websites related to crimes and set up an account. Finally, the offenders familiarize themselves with the illicit platforms by sharing similar disturbing content with other members and eventually getting access to more hardcore material and VIP status. The Dark Web's ecosystem was extensively reviewed and analyzed in *Chapter 2, An Introduction to the Dark Web*.

4. Investigate the methods law enforcement uses to detect, identify, and prosecute criminals on the Dark Web

Concerning crime on the Dark Web, there are two main sides that fight each other. On the one side are the criminals, and on the other side are law enforcement, the private sector, and the community. Law enforcement, the private sector, and the community, in their efforts to combat crimes on the Dark Web, use a variety of methods and tools to detect, identify, and prosecute criminals on the Dark Web. Some of the main tools that they use are the MEMEX project, Oracle's advanced technology, Pipl Search, traffic confirmation attack, and others. Additionally, some other methods for combating crimes on the Dark Web are sting operations and honeypot traps. Although these two methods are highly effective, they pose significant ethical dilemmas in regard to their effectiveness in protecting the victims.

5. Propose, analyze, and test a system to combat/mitigate crimes on the Dark Web more effectively

From the research that took place in the context of this book, it comes out that crimes on the Dark Web are a severe existent problem that the whole world is facing. This problem, despite the massive efforts that are made by law enforcement on a global scale for its handling, is not yet being adequately faced. On the contrary, the research of this book has shown that the problem of crimes on the Dark Web, day by day, is becoming worse.

Having in mind all this and after the extensive research of the whole problem that took place in the context of this project, it has been concluded that the introduction of a centralized system for combating/mitigating crimes on the Dark Web would be useful and necessary. For this reason, the establishment of an **International Data Hub (IDH)** is being proposed. The proposed IDH aims to create an advanced multi-disciplinary platform for the extremely severe problem of crimes on the Dark Web. The solution is information sharing across and throughout all sectors, building robust partnerships resilient to human trafficking, drug trade, and child pornography. Taking the decentralized sources—that is, law enforcement, the private sector, and the community—and forcing them into a single independent database can drastically decrease the severity of the problem and save the lives of millions of victims worldwide.

The primary goal of this research is to mitigate/combat crimes on the Dark Web as it derives from the research question, which is shown as follows.

6. To what extent can crimes conducted through the Dark Web be mitigated and/or prevented?

The proposed system (IDH) was mentioned extensively in all the previous chapters of the report. Various components of this system were described throughout the chapters, as well as how it can help to mitigate/combat crimes on the Dark Web more effectively.

This research has been devoted to investigating the Dark Web's ecosystem. Overall, this research has developed an understanding of the nature of the problem of crimes on the Dark Web and how criminals operate on this hidden part of the internet. Due to the substantial breadth of the knowledge domain, the research focused on the areas of the following cybersecurity fields:

1. Digital forensics
2. Policy, strategy, awareness, and audit
3. The legal and regulatory environment

Understanding the Dark Web can aid cybersecurity professionals, particularly those who deal directly with defending critical systems against cyberattacks, in studying the ways of the enemy.

Final tips on how to use the Dark Web

It's critical to maintain perspective. There are a lot of good reasons to use TOR, and doing so does not imply that a person is doing something risky or against the law. To encourage young people to adopt safer online behaviors, it is essential to have open and honest dialogues with them. Tell them you don't want them exposed to any of the illicit content that is prevalent on the Dark Web. Examine their reasons for wanting to use TOR and talk through all of your alternatives with them. For instance, if their goal is to increase their online anonymity, there could be other approaches you can come to an understanding on.

The freedom of the press is one political issue that many young people are worried about. To bring this topic to light and give students a safe space to ask questions and express their ideas, schools may choose to use discussions of high-profile examples such as Wikileaks. Additionally, there are certain doable actions that can be taken to provide youth with some of the security they might believe the Dark Web offers:

- Encourage young people to use privacy settings on social media, use caution when posting content online, and manage who appears on their contact and friend lists. Our privacy is affected by the information we share online and with whom we share it, as well as by things such as our internet search history. Visit the *Thinkuknow* website to learn how to manage your online life and explore methods for helping you be safe online.

- Talk about the use of **virtual private networks** (**VPNs**). People may use a VPN because they believe it will offer an extra layer of security to their online activity if they are concerned about their privacy and security. Your data is safely encrypted when utilizing a VPN, and your computer will communicate with the internet as though you are connected to a different network.

- Make sure they are aware of where to go if they encounter anything worrying or unsettling when browsing any website. Encourage them to come to you or another adult they trust if they have any concerns about anything online. Assist them in understanding how to report if they are concerned about sexual abuse and exploitation online.

Make sure you stay safe if you choose to utilize the Dark Web if you have a valid or necessary reason to do so. Here are some ways to protect yourself when you actually decide to use the Dark Web:

- **Trust your intuition**: You should safeguard yourself online to avoid falling victim to scams. Everyone is not what they seem to be. You must be cautious about who you speak with and the places you go in order to stay secure. If anything doesn't feel right, you should always act to get out of the situation.

- **Detach your online persona from real life**: Never use your login, email address, actual name, password, or even your payment card on any other website. If required, create fresh throwaway accounts and IDs for yourself. Before making any purchases, obtain prepaid debit cards that cannot be traced. Useless information about you should never be shared online or in person.

- **Employ active monitoring of identity and financial theft**: Identity protection is increasingly a common feature of internet security services for your protection. If these tools are made available to you, make sure you use them.

- **Explicitly avoid Dark Web file downloads**: The Dark Web is an area where there is no law, thus there is a lot more concern about malware infection there. In the event that you decide to download, real-time file scanning from an antivirus program might assist you in verifying any incoming files.

- **Disable ActiveX and Java in any available network settings**: These frameworks are infamous for being investigated and abused by bad actors. You should avoid this danger because you are moving via a network that is full of the aforementioned risks.

And remember—most importantly, avoid scammy websites that may put you in trouble.

Summary

In this chapter, all the objectives we covered were answered through an extensive and detailed analysis of the literature. Responses to crimes on the Dark Web are most efficient, coordinated, and practical when they are collaborative in their problem-solving. Even though the proposed system has flaws to some extent, the IDH can aid law enforcement efforts in combating Dark Web crimes. It would be useful to develop the proposed system and the overall concept by creating the necessary software. Probing deeper, the results in this research also provide a strong foundation for future research related to awareness of crimes on the Dark Web. In regard to future work, a chance to actually develop this system would be a great opportunity, although it may take a lot of time, effort, and expense. This can be done by collaborating with various international law enforcement agencies.

Index

Packt.com

Subscribe to our online digital library for full access to over 7,000 books and videos, as well as industry leading tools to help you plan your personal development and advance your career. For more information, please visit our website.

Why subscribe?

- Spend less time learning and more time coding with practical eBooks and Videos from over 4,000 industry professionals

- Improve your learning with Skill Plans built especially for you

- Get a free eBook or video every month

- Fully searchable for easy access to vital information

- Copy and paste, print, and bookmark content

Did you know that Packt offers eBook versions of every book published, with PDF and ePub files available? You can upgrade to the eBook version at packt.com and as a print book customer, you are entitled to a discount on the eBook copy. Get in touch with us at customercare@packtpub.com for more details.

At www.packt.com, you can also read a collection of free technical articles, sign up for a range of free newsletters, and receive exclusive discounts and offers on Packt books and eBooks.

Other Books You May Enjoy

If you enjoyed this book, you may be interested in these other books by Packt:

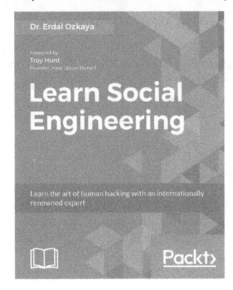

Learn Social Engineering

Dr. Erdal Ozkaya

ISBN: 9781788837927

- Learn to implement information security using social engineering

- Learn social engineering for IT security

- Understand the role of social media in social engineering

- Get acquainted with Practical Human hacking skills

- Learn to think like a social engineer

- Learn to beat a social engineer

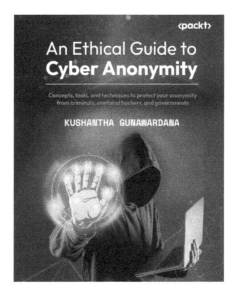

An Ethical Guide to Cyber Anonymity

Kushantha Gunawardana

ISBN: 9781801810210

- Understand privacy concerns in cyberspace
- Discover how attackers compromise privacy
- Learn methods used by attackers to trace individuals and companies
- Grasp the benefits of being anonymous over the web
- Discover ways to maintain cyber anonymity
- Learn artifacts that attackers and competitors are interested in

Packt is searching for authors like you

If you're interested in becoming an author for Packt, please visit `authors.packtpub.com` and apply today. We have worked with thousands of developers and tech professionals, just like you, to help them share their insight with the global tech community. You can make a general application, apply for a specific hot topic that we are recruiting an author for, or submit your own idea.

Share Your Thoughts

Now you've finished *Combating Crime on the Dark Web*, we'd love to hear your thoughts! Scan the QR code below to go straight to the Amazon review page for this book and share your feedback or leave a review on the site that you purchased it from.

`https://packt.link/r/1803234989`

Your review is important to us and the tech community and will help us make sure we're delivering excellent quality content.

Download a free PDF copy of this book

Thanks for purchasing this book!

Do you like to read on the go but are unable to carry your print books everywhere? Is your eBook purchase not compatible with the device of your choice?

Don't worry, now with every Packt book you get a DRM-free PDF version of that book at no cost.

Read anywhere, any place, on any device. Search, copy, and paste code from your favorite technical books directly into your application.

The perks don't stop there, you can get exclusive access to discounts, newsletters, and great free content in your inbox daily

Follow these simple steps to get the benefits:

1. Scan the QR code or visit the link below

https://packt.link/free-ebook/9781803234984

2. Submit your proof of purchase
3. That's it! We'll send your free PDF and other benefits to your email directly